THE MOVIE Murder MYSTERY QUIZ BOOK

50 Years of Whodunits

THE MOVIE Murder MYSTERY QUIZ BOOK

Dear Jerry —
Hope you enjoy
this after your
50th year!

Love,
Lucy & Ken
Julie & David

50 Years of Whodunits

JOHN M. HOWARD

SAN DIEGO • NEW YORK
A. S. BARNES & COMPANY, INC.
IN LONDON:
THE TANTIVY PRESS

First Edition
Manufactured in the United States of America

For information write to:

A.S. Barnes & Company, Inc.
P.O. Box 3051
La Jolla, California 92038

The Tantivy Press
Magdalen House
136-148 Tooley Street
London, SE1 2TT, England

Library of Congress Cataloging in Publicaton Data

Howard, John Marshall, 1922-
　　Movie murder mystery quiz book.

　　1. Detective and mystery films — Miscellanea.
I. Title.
PN1995.9.D4H6　　　　　　791.43　　　　　79-25871
ISBN 0-498-02522-5

1　2　3　4　5　6　7　8　9　　85　　84　　83　　82　　81

To Mother, Father,
and Lewis

Contents

Acknowledgments...

... to the following motion picture studios for the photos used in this book: Columbia Pictures, Eagle-Lion, MGM, Paramount, RKO Radio, Twentieth Century-Fox, United Artists, Universal-International and Warner Brothers. Thanks also to Mark Ricci of The Memory Shop for his help in the selection of illustrations; and special thanks to agent Kim Rossten, whose conscientious and untiring efforts helped make this book possible.

Introduction

Writing this book has been a labor of love.

If you're like me, there is no fun to equal that of going to the movies—unless it's the fun of asking and answering questions *about* the movies. Perhaps, like me, your favorite type of movie is the murder mystery . . . which could be one reason you're looking at this book right now!

I have made no attempt to categorize the quizzes in these pages as "easy" or "difficult." That is a matter you are free to decide for yourself. What is easy for you may be difficult for a fellow movie buff, and vice-versa. For example, you may be sharp on lethal ladies but weak on amnesia victims . . . while your fellow buff may be gung-ho on Philip Marlowe but feel "blah" about Ellery Queen.

But whether you find them hard or easy, I hope the quizzes in this book are as much fun for you to solve as they were for me to write. There is no quiz that must be done ahead of any other. This is a book you can dip into at random and enjoy equally well, whether you turn the pages forward or backward.

I cannot close without expressing appreciation to my good friend, Julian Schlossberg. I suspect that the idea for doing this book began to percolate in my mind in 1976, when Julian first made me a panelist on the "Nostalgia Night" segment of his popular radio show, "Movie Talk." Answering all kinds of movie questions called in by listeners for hours at a clip made me keenly aware of the multitudes who revel in "movie quizzery." Therefore, Julian, perhaps more than he realizes, served as a source of inspiration for this book.

I also appreciate and value highly the friendship of John Springer, whose exceptional knowledge of the movies and outstanding achievements in movie books provide a standard of excellence for anyone attempting a book on the cinema.

And I want to thank Candy Jones for her generosity in allowing me to talk my head off so many times to her radio audience on my favorite subject—the movies.

Last but not least, let me acknowledge the support and encouragement of Joe Franklin, who made nostalgia a household word.

A grateful author has fulfilled the dream of getting his idea into print. Its success, and that of any future dreams, rests with you.

John M. Howard

THE MOVIE *Murder* MYSTERY QUIZ BOOK

50 Years of Whodunits

1 Minna Gombell, William Henry, Edward Brophy
Nora and Nick Charles (Myrna Loy and William Powell)
are threatened by gangster Phil Church (Sheldon Leonard)
who is later murdered. Name this "Thin Man" film.
(answer on page 135)

How much do you really know about this popular detective series of the thirties and forties, beyond the fact that William Powell and Myrna Loy co-starred as Nick and Nora Charles, and had a pet terrier named Asta? Here are some questions regarding plots, killers, victims, suspects and other cast members that will truly test your knowledge.

Titles

To simplify your answers, here are the titles of all six pictures in the series:

(a) "The Thin Man"   (b) "Song of the Thin Man"

(c) "Shadow of the Thin Man"

(d) "Another Thin Man"   (e) "After the Thin Man"

(f) "The Thin Man Goes Home"

Answer the questions in each of the following groups by indicating (a), (b), (c), (d), (e) or (f)

Here's the Plot — Name the Picture

1. A jockey mysteriously "bites the dust" at the racetrack while Nick and Nora are there. Nick gets into the case when a reporter buddy of his is accused of killing another reporter who had been involved with gangsters and blackmail. A third killing takes place before the case is wrapped up.

2. The worthless husband of Nora's cousin is knocked off in San Francisco on New Year's Eve while carrying $25,000 worth of bonds in his pocket. Nick uncovers a blackmail plot involving a café owner and a singer with whom the deceased was infatuated. Two more murders occur before Nick unmasks the killer.

3. An eccentric inventor named Wynant mysteriously vanishes. His daughter suspects foul play and persuades Nick to help her find him. Wynant is later discovered to be a murder victim. His secretary-mistress and a gangster are also rubbed out before Nick tracks down the killer.

4. Nick and Nora are approached for help by a pair of newlyweds who are suspected of killing a bandleader on a gambling ship casino. Nick gets involved when an unseen trigger man shoots a bottle of scotch out of his hand as he is talking with the couple. The dead bandleader's blonde vocalist is also murdered in the course of the proceedings.

5. While he and Nora are visiting his parents in Sycamore Springs, Nick discovers that an artist has been bumped off, and that the victim's paintings are sought by a mysterious couple. An eccentric character named Crazy Mary is also murdered in the proceedings, during which Nick uncovers an espionage plot.

1

6. Nora's guardian is murdered on his Long Island estate while Nick and Nora are spending the weekend with him. A second murder victim is a gangster with the strange habit of dreaming that people are dead.

Here's The Killer — Name the Picture

1. Lloyd Corrigan   2. Leon Ames   3. James Stewart   4. Henry O'Neill

5. Porter Hall   6. Virginia Grey

Here Are the Victims — Name the Picture

1. Alan Baxter, Lou Lubin   2. Philip Reed, Gloria Grahame   3. C. Aubrey Smith, Sheldon Leonard

4. Alan Marshal, Paul Fix   5. Edward Ellis, Natalie Moorhead, Harold Huber   6. Anne Revere

Here Are the Suspects — Name the Picture

1. Elissa Landi, Joseph Calleia, Dorothy McNulty, George Zucco, William Law

2. Ruth Hussey, Patric Knowles, Don Costello, Harry Bellaver, Abner Biberman

3. William Bishop, Patricia Morison, Ralph Morgan, Don Taylor

4. Helen Vinson, Leon Ames, Gloria DeHaven, Edward Brophy, Donald Meek

5. Barry Nelson, Donna Reed, Stella Adler, Loring Smith, Joseph Anthony

6. Maureen O'Sullivan, Cesar Romero,

Other "Thin Man" Questions

1. In which two pictures did Nat Pendleton play Lieutenant Guild?

2. In which two pictures did Sam Levene play Lieutenant Abrams?

3. In which film did Asta become the father of pups?

4. In which movie did Keenan Wynn play a hot-lick piccolo player?

5. In which picture was Baby Nick Jr. introduced?

6. In which film did Nora reveal to Nick that she was "expecting" by coyly knitting a baby bootie in the last scene?

(answers on page 123)

2 Sidney Toler (right) as Charlie Chan and Harold Huber as a police official examine evidence in "Charlie Chan in Rio." This 1941 film was a remake of what 1931 Chan mystery? (answer on page 135)

As a seasoned murder mystery buff, you assuredly know that this famous Oriental detective has been portrayed on the screen by Warner Oland, Sidney Toler and Roland Winters. Here is an assortment of questions calculated to test the depth of your knowledge of the entire Chan series.

Titles

Name the actor (Oland, Toler or Winters) who played Charlie Chan in each of the following films:

(a) "Charlie Chan in Honolulu"

(b) "Charlie Chan's Murder Cruise"

(c) "The Chinese Ring"

(d) "Charlie Chan's Secret"

(e) "Charlie Chan in Reno"

(f) "Charlie Chan in the Secret Service"

(g) "Sky Dragon"

(h) "Charlie Chan at Treasure Island"

(i) "The Black Camel"

(j) "Charlie Chan's Chance"

(k) "Docks of New Orleans"

(l) "Charlie Chan in the City of Darkness"

(m) "Charlie Chan at the Wax Museum"

Players

Name the film in which each of these stars appeared as a supporting player. (They are all films in which Warner Oland took the role of Chan.)

1. Rita Hayworth (billed as Rita Cansino)　2. Boris Karloff

3. Bela Lugosi　4. Ray Milland　5. Robert Young　6. George Brent

Plots

In which Chan film did each of these incidents occur?

1. While aboard a train, Charlie Chan, attacked by a cobra, charms it by playing a Chinese phonograph record.

2. Chan goes backstage to apprehend an escaped lunatic who is apparently trying to murder a prima donna.

3. Charlie visits the land of the Pharaohs to investigate the disappearance of priceless treasures from the tomb of a high priest.

4. An actress named Shelah Fane is murdered in Hawaii.

5. In London, a frantic young woman prevails upon Chan to save her brother from the gallows. In sixty-five hours, the brother, who has been found guilty of murder, is to be hanged.

6. A major is murdered on a ship, but the mark of the death-dealing instrument seems to indicate that he had been kicked to death by a horse.

7. Charlie Chan assists G-men in breaking up an opium ring.

8. Charlie is called away from a testimonial dinner given in his honor by the metropolitan police, to investigate the homicide of a shady lady in a plush nightclub.

9. Detective Chan goes to Berlin to investigate the theft of a robot pilot device which has resulted in two murders.

10. Charlie unravels the mystery of attempted sabotage in the United States Fleet during a transit of the Panama Canal.

Wise Sayings

Each of the following wise sayings was spoken by Charlie Chan in one of the films listed below. Match the epigram with the film.

1. "Only a very brave mouse will make its nest in a cat's ear."

2. "Hen squats with caution on thin egg."

3. "Must turn up many stones to find hiding place of snake."

4. "Even wise fly sometimes mistake spider web for old man's whiskers."

5. "Theory, like mist on eyeglasses, obscures fact."

6. "Haste is only necessary when withdrawing one's hand from a tiger's mouth or when catching a flea."

7. "If you wish wild bird to sing, do not place him in cage."

Answer Choices for 1-7

(a) "Charlie Chan in Paris" (b) "Charlie Chan in London" (c) "Charlie Chan's Greatest Case"

(d) "Charlie Chan in Egypt" (e) "Charlie Chan's Chance" (f) "Charlie Chan's Courage"

(g) "Charlie Chan Carries On"

Other "Charlie Chan" Questions

1. Name the Chan picture in which a witness observes the illuminated dial of the killer's wrist watch during the commission of a murder in a totally dark room.

2. Name the Chan movie in which the murderer turns out to be two men who take turns wearing the same disguise, each providing an alibi for the other. One man is always present among the innocent bystanders when a murder occurs, while the other man is committing the crime.

3. Name the first talkie in which Charlie Chan was introduced as a character. (It was a Fox film released in 1929 and Chan appeared only briefly toward the end of the picture.)

4. Who was the male star of this picture?

5. Who played Charlie Chan in this movie? (It was not Warner Oland, Sidney Toler or Roland Winters.)

(answers on page 123)

3 Sherlock Holmes (Basil Rathbone, left), and Dr. Watson
(Nigel Bruce) share a tense moment of discovery in "The
Adventures of Sherlock Holmes." Who played the
feminine lead in this 1939 film? (answer on page 135)

What two actors immediately spring to mind as the best-known Sherlock Holmes and Dr. Watson in filmdom? Elementary! The answer is Basil Rathbone and Nigel Bruce. However, these two colorful Thespians had many capable predecessors and successors who played the same roles. Here are some questions designed to test your overall knowledge of Sherlock Holmes on the talking-picture screen.

Plots

Name the Rathbone-Bruce film in which the following happenings occur:

1. Holmes solves a wave of murders in which the victims are all attractive girls, each of whom, when found, is minus her right forefinger.

2. Professor Moriarty tries to steal the Crown Jewels from the Tower of London.

3. Holmes investigates murders in Musgrave Manor, a "haunted" mansion inhabited by war veterans suffering from shattered nerves.

4. On a train bound from London to Edinburgh, Holmes solves a baffling diamond robbery and the murder of the gem's owner.

5. Holmes goes to the U.S. during World War II to prevent a man named Heinrich Hinkle from obtaining a secret microfilm.

6. An eminent scientist who has invented a new bombsight is menaced by Moriarty, who is prepared to sell the device to the Nazis.

7. Holmes investigates a continuing series of killings that take place in a private club called The Good Companions.

8. To collect insurance from men who are unwisely insured, an evil group led by a woman uses rare spiders, whose bites cause unbearable pain, to drive the victims to suicide.

9. Searching for the fabulous Borgia pearl, which had been hidden in a wet-plaster bust of Napoleon, Holmes tangles with a deformed giant known as The Creeper.

10. Aboard ship, Holmes acts as a bodyguard to the heir of a throne, protecting the young king from kidnappers, spies, assassins and smugglers.

Other "Sherlock Holmes" Questions

1. Who was the first actor to play Sherlock Holmes in a talking picture (1929), and what was the title of this picture?

2. Who played Inspector Lestrade as a "regular" in the Rathbone-Bruce series?

3. Name the first picture in which Basil Rathbone took over the role of Sherlock Holmes, and name the actor who got top billing in this picture. The year was 1939.

4. Two different Sherlock Holmes films, one in 1965 and one in 1979, dealt with Jack the Ripper. The same actor played Inspector Lestrade in both pictures. Name the films, and name the actor.

5. The same actor played Sherlock Holmes in these five films: "Sherlock Holmes' Fatal Hour" (1931), "The Missing Rembrandt" (1932), "The Sign of the Four" (1932), "The Triumph of Sherlock Holmes" (1935) and "Silver Blaze" (1937). Name the actor.

6. A 1946 Sherlock Holmes film with Basil Rathbone and Nigel Bruce had the same title as an unrelated 1941 Michael Shayne film which starred Lloyd Nolan. What was the title?

7. Who played Professor Moriarty in "The Adventure of Sherlock Holmes' Smarter Brother"?

8. In what film did Ernest Torrence play Moriarty?

9. Who played Mrs. Hudson as a "regular" in the Rathbone-Bruce series?

10. Christopher Lee appeared in three Sherlock Holmes films: "The Hound of the Baskervilles" (1959), "Sherlock Holmes and the Necklace of Death" (1959) and "The Private Life of Sherlock Holmes" (1970). In each of these pictures, he played a different character. Name the role he played in each film.

11. In what 1931 picture did Raymond Massey make his screen debut in the role of Sherlock Holmes?

12. The same actor who played Dr. Watson in a 1932 film was seen as Sherlock Holmes in a film the following year. Name the actor, and name both films.

13. Name the movie in which a crazy judge (George C. Scott) who thinks he is Sherlock Holmes has an encounter with a lady psychiatrist (Joanne Woodward) named Dr. Watson.

14. Who played the roles of Holmes and Watson in "The Private Life of Sherlock Holmes"?

15. Who played the roles of Holmes and Watson in "Murder By Decree"?

16. Who played the roles of Holmes and Watson in "The Seven-Per-Cent Solution"?

17. What three actors played Moriarty in the Rathbone-Bruce series?

18. In which film did Laurence Olivier play Moriarty?

19. Alan Mowbray appeared in three Sherlock Holmes movies, each time in a different role. He played Inspector Gore-King of Scotland Yard in a 1932 film; Inspector Lestrade in a 1933 film; and Major Duncan-Bleek (who turns out to be the notorious Colonel Sebastian Moran) in a 1946 film. Name the three films.

(answers on page 124)

4 Jed Prouty and Gracie Allen in a scene from "The Gracie Allen Murder Case." With Gracie in the cast, audiences expected more comedy than mystery — and they got it! The actor who played Philo Vance had previously played that role in "The Dragon Murder Case." What was his name? (answer on page 135)

Philo Vance

A number of suave actors have portrayed that master detective, Philo Vance, on the screen. And the role of his less-than-brilliant sidekick, Sergeant Heath, has fallen to an assortment of reliable funny-men. Let's see how much you remember about Philo and his various movie adventures.

Listed below are the titles of all the Philo Vance mysteries that have appeared on the screen. To answer each of the questions that follow, simply indicate the appropriate letter (or letters) of the alphabet.

Titles

(a) "The Benson Murder Case"

(b) "The Bishop Murder Case"

(c) "Calling Philo Vance"

(d) "The Canary Murder Case"

(e) "The Casino Murder Case"

(f) "The Dragon Murder Case"

(g) "The Garden Murder Case"

(h) "The Gracie Allen Murder Case"

(i) "The Greene Murder Case"

(j) "The Kennel Murder Case"

(k) "Night of Mystery"

(l) "Philo Vance's Gamble"

(m) "Philo Vance Returns"

(n) "Philo Vance's Secret Mission"

(o) "The Scarab Murder Case"

Questions

1. In which four pictures did William Powell play Philo Vance?

2. In which two did Warren William play Vance?

3. In one film, Paul Lukas played Philo Vance, and in another, he appeared as one of the suspects. Name the two films.

4. Name the movie in which Louise Brooks played a blackmailing songbird who got murdered.

5. In what picture did a featherbrained female refer to Philo Vance as "Fido" Vance?

6. Name the film whose suspect list included Rosalind Russell, Arthur Byron, Isabel Jewell and Leslie Fenton.

7. In which film did Jean Arthur play the killer, and in which was she merely a cast member?

8. "Calling Philo Vance" was a remake of what earlier Vance mystery?

9. In which five pictures did Eugene Pallette handle the role of Sergeant Heath?

10. Name the movie in which William Demarest played Heath.

11. In which film did the group of suspects include Virginia Bruce, Benita Hume, H. B. Warner and Kent Smith?

12. In one picture, Robert Barrat played the killer, and in another, he played one of the victims. Name the two pictures.

13. In what film was Edmund Lowe seen as Philo Vance?

14. Which movie gave Basil Rathbone a crack at playing Vance?

15. Name the picture in which Mary Astor, Helen Vinson, Paul Cavanagh, Jack LaRue and Arthur Hohl were among those placed under suspicion.

16. Roscoe Karns took the role of Sergeant Heath in which picture?

17. What film cast Donald Cook in the role of the killer?

18. "Night of Mystery" was a remake of what earlier Vance mystery?

19. In which movie did Ted Healy gag his way through the role of Sergeant Heath?

20. In what two pictures did Alan Curtis portray Philo Vance?

21. What film placed James Stephenson in the part of Vance?

22. In what movie were Margaret Lindsay, Lyle Talbot, George E. Stone, Helen Lowell and Dorothy Tree among the suspects?

23. Name the picture in which Nat Pendleton was seen as Sergeant Heath.

24. Philo Vance was played by the British actor, Wilfred Hyde-White, in which film?

25. Name the movie in which the killer matched his crimes to Mother Goose rhymes.

(answers on page 124)

Perry Mason

5 The man in the middle is Ricardo Cortez in the role of Perry Mason. From which entry in the Mason detective series is this scene? (answer on page 135)

Perry Mason

Some twenty years before Raymond Burr turned up on TV as Perry Mason, Warner Brothers had pleased movie-going audiences with an unspectacular but satisfying series of whodunits featuring that same ingenious lawyer-sleuth. Let's see how knowledgeable you are with respect to the various Mason movies released during the thirties.

Titles

(a) "The Case of the Lucky Legs"

(b) "The Case of the Stuttering Bishop"

(c) "The Case of the Black Cat"

(d) "The Case of the Curious Bride"

(e) "The Case of the Howling Dog"

(f) "The Case of the Velvet Claws"

Answer each of the following questions by indicating (a), (b), (c), (d), (e) or (f):

Here's the Plot — Name the Picture

In which of the above pictures did each of these happenings occur?

1. An eccentric, bedridden millionaire named Peter Laxter is murdered. Two additional killings occur before Mason uncovers the guilty party from among half-a-dozen suspects, each of whom has hopes of sharing the Laxter estate.

2. After Perry and his beloved secretary, Della Street, are married by a lady judge, Perry is torn from his bride's arms on their wedding night and immersed in murder and evil-doings. A mysterious brunette shanghais him at gunpoint and forces him to extricate her from a blackmail scheme. During the bizarre proceedings, a man named Belter is murdered, and Mason finds himself eyed by the police as one of the suspects.

3. A man named Moxley gets married, disappears and is presumed dead. Rhoda, his "widow," remarries. When Moxley suddenly reappears out of nowhere, Rhoda doesn't believe her eyes and has his "body" exhumed. The coffin is found to contain a wooden, cigar-store Indian. Moxley attempts blackmail and becomes a permanent corpse. Rhoda is accused of the murder. Suspects include a burlesque queen whom Moxley had double-crossed; her hoodlum brother; Rhoda's jealous husband; and a doctor with whom she has been romantically involved. Mason takes the case for Rhoda's defense and finds the real killer.

4. A fly-by-night beauty contest promoter is murdered by an unknown assailant who plunges a surgeon's scalpel through his heart. Mason discovers that the fiancé of one of the cheated contest-winners is a surgeon and that the young lady herself was seen leaving the deceased's room on the night of the fatal incident. The suspects also include a second bilked contender, plus a mysterious "other woman."

5. Which was the **first** picture in the Perry Mason series?

6. Which four films featured Warren William in the role of Perry Mason?

7. In which two pictures did Claire Dodd play Perry's attractive and helpful gal Friday, Della Street?

8. In which film was Allen Jenkins cast as the gruff Sergeant Holcomb?

9. Which movie spotlighted Ricardo Cortez as Mason?

10. In which picture did Errol Flynn make his American screen debut in the role of a corpse?

11. Which movie in the series featured Ann Dvorak as Della?

12. In which two pictures did Allen Jenkins play the affable but none-too-bright Spudsy, Mason's right-hand man?

13. In which film was Genevieve Tobin seen as Della?

14. In which movie was the role of Mason handled by Donald Woods?

15. Which picture cast the same Donald Woods in the role of one of the suspects (who turned out to be the killer)?

16. In which film did Helen Trenholme play Della?

17. Which movie featured June Travis in the Della Street role?

(answers on page 125)

Bulldog Drummond

 Algy Longworth (Reginald Denny, right) is about to use his gun butt to prevent a smashing blow to the skull of his friend, Hugh Drummond (Ray Milland, left). What's the title of this "Bulldog Drummond" picture? (answer on page 135)

That dashing gentleman sleuth, Bulldog Drummond, made his presence felt a number of times on the screen. It is generally conceded that Ronald Colman was the most debonair of all the "Bulldogs." However, John Howard (to whom the author of this book is not related) holds the record for playing Drummond the greatest number of times. Interesting note: Messrs. Colman and Howard played **brothers** in the 1937 film, "Lost Horizon." Also worthy of mention is the fact that Ralph Richardson appeared in two 1935 Bulldog Drummond movies — once as Drummond, and once as a detestable villain. Here are some questions to test your knowledge of the series.

Various "Bulldogs"

Match the actors who played Bulldog Drummond (column #1) with the picture in which each actor played the role.

1. Ronald Colman   (a) "Calling Bulldog Drummond"

2. John Howard   (b) "The Return of Bulldog Drummond"

3. Richard Johnson   (c) "Bulldog Drummond's Revenge"

4. John Lodge   (d) "Deadlier Than the Male"

5. Ray Milland   (e) "Bulldog Drummond Strikes Back" (1934 film)

6. Walter Pidgeon   (f) "Bulldog Drummond Strikes Back" (1947 film)

7. Ron Randell   (g) "Bulldog Drummond At Bay" (1937 film)

8. Ralph Richardson   (h) "Bulldog Drummond Escapes"

Leading Ladies

Column #1 lists eleven attractive leading ladies (not all were heroines) of Bulldog Drummond films. Column #2 lists the films in which these actresses appeared. See how many ladies and titles you can match correctly.

1. Heather Angel   (a) "Calling Bulldog Drummond"

2. Joan Bennett   (b) "Some Girls Do"

3. Louise Campbell   (c) "Deadlier Than the Male"

4. Dahlia Lavi   (d) "Bulldog Drummond At Bay" (1937 film)

5. Margaret Leighton   (e) "Bulldog Drummond At Bay" (1947 film)

6. Anita Louise   (f) "Bulldog Drummond"

7. Dorothy Mackaill   (g) "Bulldog Drummond Comes Back"

8. Elke Sommer   (h) "Bulldog Drummond Strikes Back" (1934 film)

9. Ann Todd   (i) "Bulldog Drummond's Bride"

10. Fay Wray   (j) "The Return of Bulldog Drummond"

11. Loretta Young   (k) "Alias Bulldog Drummond" (Title in Great Britain: "Bulldog Jack")

Test Your "Nielsen" Rating

Column #1 lists four actors who played Bulldog Drummond's irascible friend, Colonel Nielsen of Scotland Yard. Match the actor with the film in which each appeared.

1. John Barrymore   (a) "Bulldog Drummond Escapes"

2. C. Aubrey Smith   (b) "Bulldog Drummond's Secret Police"

3. Sir Guy Standing   (c) "Bulldog Drummond's Peril"

4. H. B. Warner   (d) "Bulldog Drummond Strikes Back" (1934 film)

Villains

Match the villains in column #1 with the movie in which each did his dirty work.

Column #1	Column #2
1. Leo G. Carroll	(a) "Bulldog Drummond in Africa"
2. Eduardo Ciannelli	(b) "Bulldog Drummond"
3. Lawrence Grant	(c) "Bulldog Drummond's Bride"
4. Porter Hall	(d) "Arrest Bulldog Drummond"
5. J. Carrol Naish	(e) "Bulldog Drummond Strikes Back" (1934 film)
6. Warner Oland	(f) "Bulldog Drummond Escapes"
7. Ralph Richardson	(g) "Bulldog Drummond's Secret Police"
8. George Zucco	(h) "Alias Bulldog Drummond" (Title in Great Britain: "Bulldog Jack")

(answers on page 125)

7 Peter Lorre as he appeared in "Think Fast, Mr. Moto."
Can you name his leading lady in this Moto episode?
(answer on page 135)

You undoubtedly know that Peter Lorre played the title role in this detective series of the late thirties. But let's test your knowledge of the various films that comprised the series. Here are some thumbnail plot descriptions, together with corresponding supporting casts. Match these with the appropriate titles, which appear below.

Titles

(a) "Mr. Moto Takes a Vacation"   (b) "Mr. Moto Takes a Chance"   (c) "Mysterious Mr. Moto"

(d) "Mr. Moto's Gamble"   (e) "Mr. Moto's Last Warning"   (f) "Think Fast, Mr. Moto"

(g) "Thank You, Mr. Moto"

1. Moto solves the murder by poison of a prizefighter in the ring.
   (Lynn Bari, Maxie Rosenbloom, Lon Chaney Jr., Douglas Fowley, Harold Huber)

2. Moto pretends to be an archaeologist in Indochina.
   (Rochelle Hudson, Robert Kent, J. Edward Bromberg, Chick Chandler)

3. Moto gets involved with smugglers in Shanghai.
   (Virginia Field, Thomas Beck, Sig Rumann, Murray Kinnell)

4. Moto goes after a group of priceless Chinese scrolls which, when assembled, reveal a map showing the location of Genghis Khan's buried treasure.
   (Thomas Beck, Pauline Frederick, Sidney Blackmer, John Carradine, Sig Rumann)

5. Moto thwarts a conspiracy to destroy the Suez Canal.
   (George Sanders, Ricardo Cortez, John Carradine, Virginia Field)

6. Posing as an inmate at Devil's Island in order to gain the confidence of a criminal who belongs to an assassination ring, Moto helps the convict escape — then foils the lawless group in London.
   (Mary Maguire, Henry Wilcoxon, Erik Rhodes, Harold Huber, Leon Ames)

7. Moto is involved in an expedition to track down the crown of the Queen of Sheba.
   (Joseph Schildkraut, Lionel Atwill, Virginia Field, John King)

8. In which one of the above films did Keye Luke appear, playing the role of Charlie Chan's #1 son?

9. Many years later, Mr. Moto attempted a screen comeback. Name the actor who played the title role in "The Return of Mr. Moto," in 1965.

(answers on page 125)

 Who is the surprised gentleman confronted by Margaret Rutherford as Jane Marple in this scene from "Murder at the Gallop"? Here's a hint: he was her real-life husband. (answer on page 135)

Miss Jane Marple

This indomitable lady detective was played four times on the screen by the delightful British character actress, Margaret Rutherford. In each of her exploits, Miss Marple solemnly goes about the business of trapping the killer, undismayed by the many red herrings that are strewn in her path. Here are brief descriptions of her four screen adventures. See if you can match them with the titles below.

Titles

(a) "Murder Most Foul"   (b) "Murder Ahoy!"

(c) "Murder She Said"

(d) "Murder at the Gallop"

1. While aboard a train, Miss Marple sees a girl being strangled on a passing train.

2. Miss Marple discovers who killed a couple of people involved in an inheritance.

3. Convinced that a villager on trial for murder is innocent, Miss Marple, a jury member, hangs the jury and joins an acting troupe to expose the real murderer.

4. Miss Marple, a suspicious trustee on a training ship used for rehabilitating juvenile delinquents, comes upon embezzlement and murder.

(answers on page 125)

9 There's trouble outside for William Gargan as Ellery Queen. Who is the actress with him, and from which entry in Columbia's "Ellery Queen" series is this scene? (answer on page 135)

Titles

(a) "Ellery Queen and the Murder Ring"

(b) "A Desperate Chance for Ellery Queen"

(c) "Enemy Agents Meet Ellery Queen"

(d) "Ellery Queen, Master Detective"

(e) "Ellery Queen's Penthouse Mystery"

(f) "A Close Call for Ellery Queen"

(g) "Ellery Queen and the Perfect Crime"

1. Ralph Bellamy and William Gargan each played Ellery Queen several times on the screen. In which films did Bellamy play the role, and in which did Gargan play the role?

2. Name the actress who played Ellery Queen's secretary-companion, Nikki Porter, in all of the above films.

3. What actor played Ellery's father, Inspector Queen, in all seven films?

4. Name the actor who took the role of Inspector Velie throughout the above series.

5. Who played Ellery Queen in "The Spanish Cape Mystery"?

6. Who played Ellery Queen in "The Mandarin Mystery"?

(answers on page 126)

 George Sanders (center) made his final appearance as The Saint in this 1941 film. In the story, his mission is to deliver several rare postage stamps to Wendy Barrie. Three murders complicate his task. Can you name the movie? (answer on page 135)

This smooth, enigmatic enemy of corruption has been portrayed on the screen by three different actors: Louis Hayward, George Sanders and Hugh Sinclair. See if you know which actor played the role in each of the following films in the series:

Titles

1. "The Saint's Double Trouble"
2. "The Saint's Girl Friday"
3. "The Saint in London"
4. "The Saint in New York"
5. "The Saint in Palm Springs"
6. "The Saint Meets the Tiger"
7. "The Saint Takes Over"
8. "The Saint Strikes Back"
9. "The Saint's Vacation"

(answers on page 126)

11 Against his better judgment, The Falcon (Tom Conway) returns to Luisa Braganza (Madge Meredith) a formula for synthetic diamonds which a gang of crooks is trying to steal. In which Falcon film does this scene occur? (answer on page 135)

The Falcon

The role of this suave upholder of the law has been played on the screen by two different actors. George Sanders began the series with "The Gay Falcon," "A Date with the Falcon" and "The Falcon Takes Over." In the fourth episode, "The Falcon's Brother," he was conveniently killed and replaced by his real-life brother, Tom Conway. Here are nine Falcon films and their nine leading ladies. See if you can match the ladies and titles.

1. "A Date with the Falcon"   (a) Lynn Bari

2. "The Falcon's Adventure"   (b) Wendy Barrie

3. "The Falcon's Brother"   (c) Jean Brooks

4. "The Falcon in Danger"   (d) Rita Corday

5. "The Falcon in Hollywood"   (e) Barbara Hale

6. "The Falcon in Mexico"   (f) Harriet Hilliard

7. "The Falcon in San Francisco"   (g) Mona Maris

8. "The Falcon Strikes Back"   (h) Madge Meredith

9. "The Falcon Takes Over"   (i) Jane Randolph

(answers on page 126)

12 Edna May Oliver as Hildegarde Withers exchanges grimaces with James Gleason in the role of Inspector Piper. Give the title of this entry in the Withers-Piper series. Clue: Bruce Cabot played the killer. (answer on page 135)

The adventures of a caustic schoolmarm (Hildegarde Withers) and a bullheaded detective (Inspector Piper) provided one of the better mystery series of the thirties. Audiences enjoyed the amusing by-play between these two widely contrasting types as they set about solving crimes together.

Here are the titles of the six entries in the series. To answer the questions below, simply indicate the appropriate letter (or letters) of the alphabet.

Titles

(a) "Forty Naughty Girls"
(b) "Murder on a Bridle Path"
(c) "Penguin Pool Murder"
(d) "Murder on a Honeymoon"
(e) "The Plot Thickens"
(f) "Murder on the Blackboard"

1. In which three of the above films did Edna May Oliver play Miss Withers?

2. In which two films did fluttery ZaSu Pitts take over the role?

3. In which film was acerbic Helen Broderick seen as Hildegarde?

4. In which of the above films did James Gleason play Inspector Piper?

5. In which film was a man murdered by a hatpin stuck in his eardrum?

6. Which film dealt with the backstage death of a press agent?

(answers on page 126)

13 Reformed cracksman Michael Lanyard (also known as The Lone Wolf) uses his talents to aid the law in "The Lone Wolf Spy Hunt." Name this mustachioed actor who played the title role. Who is his wide-eyed lady friend? (answers on page 135)

Here is a list of detective-movie characters that have been played by different performers. Following each name are the names of several players, all of whom **except one** appeared in the role. Your job is to pick the one performer in each group who did **not** play the role.

1. **Torchy Blaine:** Lynn Bari, Glenda Farrell, Lola Lane, Jane Wyman

2. **Father Brown:** Walter Connolly, Alec Guinness, Michael Wilding

3. **Mike Hammer:** Robert Bray, Biff Elliott, Lee Marvin, Ralph Meeker, Mickey Spillane

4. **The Lone Wolf:** Melvyn Douglas, Tom Helmore, Francis Lederer, Gerald Mohr, Ron Randell, Warren William

5. **Arsene Lupin:** John Barrymore, Melvyn Douglas, Charles Korvin, Edmund Lowe

6. **Philip Marlowe:** Humphrey Bogart, James Garner, Elliott Gould, Robert Mitchum, George Montgomery, Robert Montgomery, Dick Powell, George Segal

7. **Hercule Poirot:** Albert Finney, Tony Randall, Michael Rennie, Peter Ustinov

8. **Michael Shayne:** Hugh Beaumont, Lloyd Nolan, Michael O'Shea

9. **Nero Wolfe:** Edward Arnold, Walter Connolly, Adolphe Menjou

10. **Mr. Wong:** Boris Karloff, Peter Lorre, Bela Lugosi

(answers on page 126)

 A pensive Warner Baxter had the title role in "Crime Doctor." This was the lead-off entry in a successful Columbia series made in the forties. Can you name the leading lady in this first episode? She had previously served two Ellery Queens very diligently. (answer on page 135)

Name the creator of each of the following fictional
detective characters that have appeared on the screen:

1. Father Brown

2. Charlie Chan

3. Nick Charles

4. Thatcher Colt

5. The Crime Doctor (Dr. Ordway)

6. Bulldog Drummond

7. The Falcon

8. Mike Hammer

9. Sherlock Holmes

10. Nurse Sarah Keate

11. The Lone Wolf (Michael Lanyard)

12. Philip Marlowe

13. Jane Marple

14. Perry Mason

15. Mr. Moto

16. Miss Pinkerton

17. Hercule Poirot

18. Ellery Queen

19. The Saint (Simon Templar)

20. Michael Shayne

21. Sam Spade

22. Philo Vance

23. Hildegarde Withers

24. Nero Wolfe

(answers on page 126)

15 Joseph Cotten intends no good by "the laying on of hands," and Teresa Wright is up to her neck in trouble, in this tense scene from "Shadow of a Doubt." What theme song runs through this picture? (answer on page 135)

When it comes to ingenious ways of creating suspense on the screen, Alfred Hitchcock has no peer. Here are some questions regarding various crimes, killers, victims, suspects, clues, motives, locales, climaxes, plot twists and casts of Hitchcock thrillers. How many can you answer correctly?

Similar Opening Scenes

1. As the picture opens, a woman's nude body is found floating down the river with a necktie around her throat, indicating that she is the latest victim of a sex-crazed, homicidal maniac. What's the movie?

2. As the picture opens, a woman's body is washed ashore, along with the belt of a man's raincoat, suggesting that she had been strangled rather than drowned. What's the movie?

Bizarre Happenings

Name the picture in which:

(a) A misplaced state document is used as a hamburger napkin.

(b) An old Dutch windmill turns in the wrong direction.

(c) A beautiful woman changes her appearance and identity every time she cracks a safe.

(d) A fugitive girl carrying a stolen bankroll checks into an eerie motel — but she never checks out!

(e) A woman refuses to drink a glass of milk her husband has given her because she believes it contains poison.

(f) A professor reveals himself to be the head of a spy ring by showing that he has a finger joint missing.

(g) A priest listens to a man confess to a murder; but bound to silence by the seal of the confessional, the clergyman is prevented from defending himself when accused of the crime.

(h) A husband's attempt to get his wife murdered backfires when she kills her would-be assassin in self-defense.

(i) An attractive girl who has an unpleasant encounter with a young lawyer in a pet shop is later attacked by a vicious seagull.

(j) The presumed leader of an international peace organization turns out to be a Nazi conspirator.

(k) A fake clairvoyant and her cab-driver accomplice clash with a jeweler and his girlfriend who kidnap people for ransoms of oversized diamonds.

(l) A man named George Kaplan is "invented" by U.S. Intelligence agents.

(answers on page 127)

Spine-Chilling Suspense

Give the title of the film in which:

1. A small boy dawdles along London streets carrying a package which, unbeknown to him, contains a time bomb.

2. Bottles in a wine cellar are found to contain uranium ore instead of wine.

3. A killer retrieves a tiepin from the clenched fingers of his victim by breaking the corpse's fingers.

4. The crash of cymbals at a particular moment during a symphonic concert signals the intended assassination of a diplomat.

5. A woman's death is reflected through the lenses of her eyeglasses, which fall to the ground as she is murdered in an amusement park.

6. A man known as "The Merry Widow Murderer" tries to push his niece off a speeding train.

Cold-Blooded Murders

Name the movie in which:

(a) Two men murder a third man "just for kicks," hide his body in a large chest, and try to maintain their cool when guests arrive for a cocktail party in the same room where the corpse is concealed.

(b) A tourist suspected of being a spy is shoved from the peak of a Swiss Alp by a Mexican assassin, who later learns that he killed the wrong man.

(c) An unbalanced playboy makes a murder pact with a tennis star. In exchange for having his father killed by the tennis player, the playboy agrees to murder the athlete's estranged wife.

Heart-Pounding Climaxes

Identify the film whose climax takes place:

1. On the wing of a wrecked transatlantic plane in mid-ocean.

2. Atop the Statue of Liberty.

3. On the giant faces of the Presidents sculptured on Mount Rushmore.

Casts

Pick the one player who was **not** in the cast of each of the following films:

(a) "Rebecca" — Laurence Olivier, Joan Fontaine, George Sanders, Judith Anderson, Charles Coburn, Nigel Bruce, Gladys Cooper, Reginald Denny

(b) "Vertigo" — James Stewart, Kim Novak, Barbara Bel Geddes, Wendell Corey, Tom Helmore

16 In "Psycho," Marion Crane (Janet Leigh) runs off with forty thousand dollars she has stolen, never dreaming of the violent and tragic consequences to be triggered by her crime. Who played the millionaire she robs? (answer on page 135)

(c) "Spellbound" — Ingrid Bergman, Gregory Peck, Rhonda Fleming, Sir Cedric Hardwicke, Michael Chekhov, Norman Lloyd, Leo G. Carroll

(d) "The Lady Vanishes" — Michael Redgrave, Margaret Lockwood, Paul Lukas, Lilli Palmer, Dame May Whitty, Cecil Parker

(e) "The Trouble With Harry" — Shirley MacLaine, Edmund Gwenn, John Forsythe, Mildred Natwick, Martin Balsam, Mildred Dunnock

(f) "The Paradine Case" — Gregory Peck, Ann Todd, Alida Valli, Charles Laughton, Louis Jourdan, Ethel Barrymore, Louis Calhern

(g) "Rear Window" — James Stewart, Grace Kelly, Thelma Ritter, Raymond Burr, Judith Evelyn, Barry Sullivan

General Questions

1. Who played the title role in "Saboteur"?

2. In what 1930 Hitchcock film did Herbert Marshall play the leading role?

3. Name the actor who appeared in more Hitchcock films than any other actor.

4. In what 1936 Hitchcock film did Robert Young play a spy?

5. In what 1940 Hitchcock movie did Edmund Gwenn play a hired assassin who accidentally falls to his death while trying to push the hero off the roof of a building?

6. Hitchcock made his first talkie in 1929. What was the title?

7. Who played the killer in "Stage Fright"?

(answers on page 127)

Academy Award Winners & Nominees

17 "Crossfire," a 1947 Academy Award nominee for best picture, presented an indictment of anti-Semitism in the form of a murder mystery. Can you identify the partially-seen killer and his victim? (answer on page 135)

Academy Award Winners & Nominees

1. Each of these Academy Award winners starred in a movie containing the word "Missing" in the title. Name the movies.
   (a) Bette Davis
   (b) Laurence Olivier
   (c) Victor McLaglen

2. William Powell receive a best-actor nomination in 1934 for "The Thin Man," and the film itself was among the nominees for best movie. Also nominated for an Oscar was the film's director. What was his name?

3. Which two cast members of "Gaslight" — one in a starring role and one in a supporting role — were nominated for, but did not win Oscars in 1944?

4. What 1940 film, directed by Alfred Hitchcock, was nominated for, but did not win, an Academy Award?

5. What player in this same 1940 Hitchcock movie was nominated for, but did not win, a best-supporting-actor Oscar?

6. Name the 1940 Hitchcock movie which **did** win the Academy Award for best picture.

7. What three players in this same 1940 Hitchcock film — two in starring roles, and one in a supporting role — were nominated for, but did not win Oscars?

8. Name five players in "Death on the Nile" who won Oscars previously for other movies.

9. For what 1952 suspense movie was Joan Crawford given an Oscar nomination?

10. What actor was also nominated for an Oscar — in the supporting category — for this same 1952 Crawford movie? (He actually had quite a big role.)

11. For what 1968 movie did Ruth Gordon win a best-supporting-actress Oscar?

12. An outstanding 1957 courtroom whodunit received Academy Award nominations in the best-picture, best-actor, best-supporting-actress and best-director categories. Name the movie.

13. Name the 1944 baffler for which supporting actor Clifton Webb and director Otto Preminger both received Oscar nominations?

14. For what 1954 film did Alfred Hitchcock receive best-director nomination?

15. For what 1944 movie and what 1948 movie — both murder melodramas rich in suspense — did Barbara Stanwyck receive best-actress nominations?

16. The director of the 1944 Stanwyck movie referred to above, actually **won** the Oscar for that movie. Who is he?

17. What supporting actor in "Spellbound" (1945) was an Oscar nominee but not a winner?

18. Name the 1940 murder melodrama for which Bette Davis was nominated as best actress.

19. What supporting actor in this same 1940 Bette Davis film also received an Oscar nomination? (He was an actor of great promise who unfortunately died shortly afterward, just as his career was beginning to flourish.)

20. Name the distinguished director who won an Oscar nomination for this same Bette Davis movie in 1940.

21. Name the 1962 shocker for which Bette Davis received an Academy Award nomination.

22. What supporting actor in this same 1962 Bette Davis film was also nominated for an Oscar?

23. Name the actress who won a best-supporting-actress nomination for her work in a 1960 Hitchcock classic.

24. A 1959 courtroom whodunit received Oscar nominations in the best-movie and best-actor categories. In addition, two actors in the film were nominated in the best-supporting-actor category. Name the movie.

25. Robert Ryan and Gloria Grahame each received a supporting Oscar nomination for what 1947 murder melodrama?

26. For what film did Agnes Moorehead receive a best-supporting-actress nomination in 1964?

18 Danny (Robert Montgomery) intimidates Olivia (Rosalind Russell) in the 1937 version of "Night Must Fall." The actor who played Danny in the 1964 remake won a 1974 Oscar nomination for best actor. Name this player, and name the 1974 movie. (answer on page 135)

49

19 Black detective Sidney Poitier earns the respect of Southern bigot Rod Steiger as they set about tracking down a killer in "In the Heat of the Night." Who directed this film? (answer on page 135)

27. A 1974 murder mystery (which took place back in the thirties) was nominated for, but did not win, Academy Awards in the best-movie, best-actor and best-actress categories. It **did** win an Oscar, however, for best original screenplay. Name the movie.

28. The two male costars (both British) and the director of what 1972 mystery melodrama, based on an enormously successful play, all received Oscar nominations?

29. For what two whodunits — in 1946 and 1947, respectively — did Ethel Barrymore receive supporting Oscar nominations?

30. Two cast members in a 1945 Oscar-nominated movie received best-supporting-actress nominations, but neither was a winner. The female star of that movie, however, **did** win an Oscar. Who were the two supporting actresses?

31. Name the 1974 movie for which an actress who had previously won two best-actress Oscars, won again — but this time in the best-supporting-actress category.

32. What actor, who had previously been known as a light comedian and romantic leading man, won an Oscar nomination for playing a murderer in a 1937 film? It was based on an Emlyn Williams play.

33. What distinguished British actress won a supporting Oscar nomination for her work in this same 1937 film? (She played a crotchety old lady who became a murder victim.)

34. The movie that won the 1967 Academy Award was a murder mystery with a built-in racial angle. It dealt with a black detective from the North who becomes a murder suspect while passing through a Southern town. After proving his innocence, he is forced to work on the case with the extremely bigoted police chief. Name (a) the movie; (b) the Oscar-winning co-star; and (c) the film's two sequels, whose central character was the black detective, Virgil Tibbs.

(answers on page 128)

20 Ida Lupino, Elsa Lanchester, Louis Hayward and Edith Barrett exchange meaningful glances in "Ladies in Retirement." Who played the mistress of the house who gets murdered in this leisurely spun tale of blackmail and homicide? (answer on page 135)

1. The 1941 classic, "The Maltese Falcon," was a remake of a 1931 film which had the same title. The same story was also done in a much-altered version in 1936 under a different title. In the 1936 version, the character played by Sydney Greenstreet in 1941 was changed to a woman. (a) In the 1931 version, who played the Humphrey Bogart, Mary Astor and Greenstreet roles? (b) Who played the corresponding roles in the 1936 version? (c) What was the title of the 1936 version?

2. "The Mystery of the Wax Museum," made in 1933, told the bloodcurdling story of a mad scientist who arranges to have bodies stolen from the morgue so that he can fashion them into wax figures for his museum. The film was remade in 1953 as "House of Wax." Who played the misguided modeler in each version?

3. Edmund Lowe starred in the 1935 original, and Ralph Bellamy in the 1942 remake, of a World War I mystery melodrama based on an E. Phillips Oppenheim novel. Each actor played the dual role of a German spy who poses as his exact physical counterpart, an English nobleman. Both versions had the same title. What was it?

4. In a 1941 shocker called "Ladies in Retirement," Ida Lupino played a housekeeper who installs two batty relatives in the home of her employer, an elderly widow — with murder resulting. The film was remade under a different title in 1969, with some plot details slightly altered. What was the remake called, and who played the Lupino role?

5. The Agatha Christie mystery, **Ten Little Indians,** was made into a 1945 movie under the title, "And Then There Were None." It was remade twice — in 1966 and 1975 — under the original title. In scrambled order, column #1 below lists the cast of version #1; column #2 lists the cast of version #2; and column #3 lists the cast of version #3. Match the performers in versions #2 and #3 with the performer who played the same role in version #1.

Column #1	Column #2	Column #3
(a) C. Aubrey Smith	Fabian	Herbert Lom
(b) June Duprez	Leo Genn	Oliver Reed
(c) Judith Anderson	Hugh O'Brian	Maria Rohm
(d) Barry Fitzgerald	Shirley Eaton	Charles Aznavour
(e) Roland Young	Dennis Price	Stephane Audran
(f) Walter Huston	Wilfred Hyde-White	Adolfo Celi
(g) Louis Hayward	Dahlia Lavi	Gert Froebe
(h) Mischa Auer	Mario Adorf	Albert de Mendoza
(i) Queenie Leonard	Marianne Hoppe	Elke Sommer
(j) Richard Haydn	Stanley Holloway	Richard Attenborough

6. George Raft, Edward Arnold and Ray Milland appeared in the 1935 original version of a Dashiell Hammett murder mystery. Arnold played a political boss, Raft was his loyal right-hand man and Milland turned up briefly as a worthless young man who got murdered. Who played the corresponding roles in the 1942 remake of the same title, and what was the title?

7. "The Mystery of Mr. X" (1934) starred Robert Montgomery as a jewel thief in London, where an outbreak of homicide has claimed the lives of several policemen. Suspected of the killings because he had stolen a diamond near the scene of the crime, Montgomery has no choice but to find the real killer — and he does! Who played Montgomery's role in the 1952 remake, and what was the title of the later version?

8. In a 1937 murder-mystery farce, Carole Lombard played the role of a compulsive liar who pleads guilty to a murder she didn't commit in a misguided attempt to advance the career of her lawyer husband. Betty Hutton played the same role in a 1946 remake which had a different title. (a) Name the 1937 original and the 1946 remake. (b) Who played the husband in each version?

9. Hitchcock's "Shadow of a Doubt" was remade in 1958 with Charles Drake, Colleen Miller and Rod Taylor in the roles originally played by Joseph Cotten, Teresa Wright and Macdonald Carey. What was the title of the remake?

10. In the 1932 original, Henry Stephenson played a doctor who murders his unfaithful wife and rigs the evidence so that her lover is accused of the crime. Edmund Lowe and Victor McLaglen played the reporter and detective, respectively, who crack the case. In the 1937 remake (which had a different title), John Barrymore played the doctor, Lynne Overman the reporter, and Charles Bickford the detective. Give the title of each version.

11. Betty Grable starred in a 1941 mystery in which Carole Landis played the murder victim and Laird Cregar played a crazed detective. The picture was remade in 1953 with a new title. (a) What was the title of the original? (b) What was the title of the remake? (c) Who played the Grable, Landis and Cregar roles in the remake?

12. Red Skelton made a big hit in 1941 when he starred in an MGM comedy mystery called "Whistling in the Dark." He played a mystery story writer who gets involved in real crime. (a) Who played Red's role originally in MGM's 1933 version of the same title? (b) Who played the villain in the 1933 version? (c) Who played the villain in the 1941 remake?

13. "Night Must Fall" was the horrifying study of a psychopathic killer named Danny, who carries with him the head of one of his victims in a hatbox. The original was filmed in 1937; it was remade in 1964. (a) Who played the unbalanced protagonist in the 1964 remake? (b) In the 1964 version, who played the invalid old lady whom Danny murders? (c) In the 1937 original, who played the old lady's timid niece who is attracted to Danny in spite of herself?

14. "Love From a Stranger" was another murder melodrama about a psychopathic killer. This time, the lethal gent is a modern Bluebeard who charms an unsuspecting sweepstakes winner into marriage and then plots to do away with her. It was filmed first in 1937, and again in 1947 with the same title. (a) Who played the killer and his potential victim in the original? (b) Who played these roles in the remake?

15. Two private-eye movies (one in 1942, the other in 1947) were based on the same Raymond Chandler novel, **The High Window.** Both films dealt with a ring of rare-coin counterfeiters and a series of murders linked to the theft of a particularly valuable coin. The 1942 film was fashioned into a Michael Shayne adventure; in the 1947 film, the sleuthing was done by Philip Marlowe. (a) Who played Shayne in the 1942 film? (b) Who played Marlowe in the 1947 film? (c) Give the titles of both movies.

16. Do these ingredients sound familiar? A gloomy mansion...thunder and lightning... a black-cloaked killer with clutching hands... a fishy-eyed butler who gets chloroformed... a $100,000 insurance policy on a dead man ...an old lady's sleeping potion spiked with arsenic...an evil-looking doctor...a spiritistic housekeeper...an invalid mother who hides incriminating evidence under her pillow. All these and more were found in a 1932 whodunit which starred private nurse Joan Blondell and detective sergeant George Brent. This picture set the pattern for later mystery films in which the detective was constantly outsmarted by his shrewder amateur sleuth lady companion. (a) Name this movie, which was based on a Mary Roberts Rinehart story. (b) What was the title of the 1941 remake?

17. Remember this 1934 movie? William Powell played a lawyer married to Myrna Loy. Learning that he's had an affair with Rosalind Russell, Myrna retaliates by having a flirtation with Harvey Stephens, who winds up blackmailing her. During a struggle with Stephens in which she tries to retrieve some incriminating letters, a shot is fired. Charged with Stephens' murder, Myrna is defended by Powell, who proves in court that someone else fired the fatal shot. (a) Name the movie. (b) Name the 1939 remake. (c) Who played the Powell-Loy roles in the remake?

18. Norma Shearer's first talkie was "The Trial of Mary Dugan" (1929), a sensational (at that time) courtroom drama about a girl who is saved from paying the penalty for a crime she did not commit. The picture was remade in 1941 with the same title. (a) Who played Mary's defender in the 1929 version? (b) Who played her prosecutor in the first version? (c) Who played Mary in the 1941 remake? (d) Who played her defender in the 1941 version? (e) Who played the prosecutor in the later version?

21 Barry Fitzgerald and Walter Huston "pool" their wits to solve the murders of their fellow house-guests in "And Then There Were None." Name the famous French director of this picture. (answer on page 135)

19. A 1938 Mr. Moto film which starred Peter Lorre was a remake of "Murder in Trinidad" (1934), and was in turn remade under the title, "The Caribbean Mystery" (1945). All three movies were based on a novel by John W. Vandercook. In the cast of the Moto film were Jean Hersholt, Leon Ames, Robert Lowery and Richard Lane. What was the title?

20. "Kind Lady" was first filmed in 1935 and remade in 1951 under the same title. It told of an unscrupulous artist who gets inside the home of a charitable lady by pleading poverty, and then holds her captive while he robs her of her possessions. (a) Who played these two roles in the original version? (b) Who enacted the two leads in the remake?

21. Alfred Hitchcock's popular 1935 suspense film, "The 39 Steps," was remade in 1960 and again in 1980 by other directors. (a) Who played the male and female leads in the original version? (b) Who played these roles in the 1960 remake?

22. There have been three screen versions of the novel, **Farewell, My Lovely**, in which the leading character was private eye Philip Marlowe. The first screen version (1942) was fashioned into a vehicle for another detective character, The Falcon, and had a title different from the novel's. The second screen version (1944) used Marlowe as the central character but also had a title different from the novel's. The third screen version (1975) had the same title as the novel and used Marlowe as the central character. (a) What was the title of the 1942 version, and who played The Falcon? (b) What was the title of the 1944 version, and who played Philip Marlowe? (c) Who played Philip Marlowe in the 1975 version? (d) Who played the brutal giant, Moose Malloy, in each of the three versions?

23. "The Big Sleep" told the complex story of an aging and ailing millionaire who hires private eye Philip Marlowe to rescue his two irresponsible daughters (the older one a headstrong divorcée, the younger one a nymphomaniac) from the clutches of blackmailers. The picture was first filmed in 1945, and remade under the same title in 1978. (a) Who played Marlowe in each version? (b) Who played the father in each version? (c) Who played the two daughters in the original? (d) Who played the two daughters in the remake?

24. "The Gorilla" was a classic mystery-thriller comedy that survived three screen versions. The first version was a 1927 silent film. Interestingly enough, Walter Pidgeon, who played in this version, also appeared in the first talkie version (1931). Can you name the wacky comedy trio that starred in the third version in 1939?

25. Bayard Veiller's spiritualist stage chiller, "The Thirteenth Chair," was filmed by MGM in two talkie versions — first in 1929, and then in 1937. It dealt with the unmasking of a murderer during a séance. The leading role was that of the medium who conducted the séances. (a) Name the actress who played the medium in the 1929 version. She had also played the role previously on the stage. (b) Who played the medium in the 1937 version?

(answers on page 129)

22 Prosecutor Dana Andrews (left, standing) stages a courtroom demonstration to establish the innocence of defendant Arthur Kennedy (seated at right in first row). Name the movie and the director. (answer on page 135)

Plot Capsules

Identify the movie from each of the following plot descriptions:

1. Prosecutor Dana Andrews becomes convinced of defendant Arthur Kennedy's innocence and proceeds to prove him not guilty of murdering a priest.

2. Art collector Clifton Webb, with the help of hoodlum William Bendix, tries to pin a phony murder rap on private eye Mark Stevens.

3. Psychopathic detective Laird Cregar, hopelessly in love with waitress Carole Landis, tries to pin her murder on promoter Victor Mature.

4. Detective George Raft discovers that actress Ginger Rogers is the killer of blackmailer Peggy Ann Garner.

5. Actress Rosalind Russell kills producer Leon Ames in a fit of rage and is stalked by suspicious police captain Sydney Greenstreet.

6. Beautiful and ruthless Joan Fontaine, eager to marry wealthy Herbert Marshall, plots to poison her husband, Richard Ney, and fasten the blame on her lover, Patric Knowles, who is Ney's doctor.

7. From her apartment window, Barbara Stanwyck sees George Sanders commit a murder, but cannot convince detective Gary Merrill that she's in her right mind, when she tells him about it.

8. Humphrey Bogart murders his wife (Rose Hobart) because his affections have turned to her younger sister (Alexis Smith).

9. A doctor (Anthony Quinn), believing himself in love with the wife (Lana Turner) of his terminally ill patient (Lloyd Nolan), plots with her to put the man out of the way by means of a fatal injection.

10. Barbara Stanwyck, a bedridden invalid, accidentally overhears her own murder being plotted over the telephone.

11. Barbara Stanwyck has a recurring dream in which a stranger tries to entice her away from her sightless spouse. When the husband mysteriously vanishes, the stranger pops up in another nightmare and takes her to a funeral chapel. There he tries to force her to marry him, while a grotesque model of her husband waits to attack her. Her nerves wrecked and no longer able to separate dreams from reality, Barbara is helped (so she thinks) by her husband's attorney, Robert Taylor.

12. George Sanders, a hen-pecked brother, plots to do away with one of his domineering sisters so that he will be free to marry Ella Raines.

13. A psychology professor (Edward G. Robinson) accidentally meets the model (Joan Bennett) of a painting he happens to be admiring in an art-store window. She invites him to her apartment, where he becomes involved in the murder of her jealous boyfriend (Dan Duryea).

14. The body of a powerful and hated industrialist (Orson Welles) is found at his country estate, with all evidence pointing to suicide. A private investigator (Michael Wilding) uncovers the truth by examining the motives of the deceased's secretary (John McCallum), his widow (Margaret Lockwood), and her uncle (Miles Malleson).

15. A diamond heiress (Anne Baxter) retreats to her villa in Spain after the tragic deaths of her father and brother. A stranger (Richard Todd) appears, producing evidence that he is her brother. Anne finds that her trusted uncle (Alexander Knox) is in league with Todd to force her into making a will signing over her estate to them. The ending reveals some startling truths.

 Joan Fontaine murders one man and makes two others miserable in this Edwardian shocker. Here she takes the stand, prepared to give perjured testimony against her lover. Can you name the film? (answer on page 135)

16. Farah Fawcett and Jeff Bridges meet by chance in New York, fall in love at first sight, get stuck with her dead husband on their hands and finally clear themselves of suspicion.

17. While investigating the disappearance of her roommate in London, an American taxi dancer (Lucille Ball) is recruited by a Scotland Yard inspector (Charles Coburn) to be the bait in trapping a modern Bluebeard who specializes in killing pretty girls. The murderer advertises for his victims in the personal columns of newspapers, and Lucy's job is to learn his identity by answering the ads.

18. Using her boss's car, an English girl (Samantha Eggar), who works in a Paris advertising agency, drops off the boss (Oliver Reed) and his wife (Stephane Audran) at the airport for a trip to Geneva. The girl, who is nearsighted and wears prescription sunglasses, then decides to take the car on a Mediterranean holiday. When a corpse turns up in the car trunk, accompanied by a gun, she is accused of the murder because her dark glasses convince witnesses along the way that they have seen her before.

19. A Colonel (C. Aubrey Smith) in the British Lancers is court-martialed and cashiered from the service. He is murdered before he can present proof of a conspiracy against him. His sons (Richard Greene, George Sanders, David Niven and William Henry) set out to clear his name and find the killer.

20. Sixteen years after the kidnapping and apparent death of his wife and child during a futile rescue attempt, a new Orleans businessman (Cliff Robertson) goes to Italy where he meets a young Italian girl (Genevieve Bujold) who is the image of the wife he believes to be dead.

21. A blind girl (Mia Farrow) is pursued by an unknown killer who has already murdered her uncle, aunt and cousin. The audience recognizes the killer by his boots but does not discover his identity until the final scene.

22. Elizabeth Taylor, the wealthy wife of stockbroker Laurence Harvey, becomes terrified by the empty old house next door because she imagines she has seen a pair of gory corpses through the window.

(answers on page 129)

24 Terrorized by a chronic telephone caller who keeps threatening her life, Doris Day becomes a bundle of nerves in "Midnight Lace." Here, she is comforted by John Gavin, who works on a building next-door to her apartment. Who played her aunt in this picture? (answer on page 135)

Title-Role Quiz

Name the murder, mystery or suspense film that co-starred each of the following pairs.

Titles

1. "Julia" and "The Graduate"

2. "Ivy" and "The Third Man"

3. "Lydia" and "Uncle Harry"

4. "Judith" and "The Man in the Gray Flannel Suit"

5. "Thelma Jordan" and "Captain Eddie"

6. "My Fair Lady" and "Mr. Lucky"

7. "Cynthia" and "Alice Adams"

8. "The Old Maid" and "The Heiress"

9. "Mildred Pierce" and "The Man in the Attic"

10. "Johnny Belinda" and "The Scarlet Empress"

11. "The Flame of New Orleans" and "Jesse James"

12. "Stella Dallas" and "The Wrong Man"

13. "Daisy Kenyon" and "The Iron Man" (1951)

14. "The Gorgeous Hussy" and "The Happiest Millionaire"

15. "The Bishop's Wife" and "The Great Garrick"

16. "Cleopatra" (1963) and "Ivanhoe"

17. "Sylvia Scarlett" and "Quentin Durward"

18. "The Barefoot Contessa" and "The Birdman of Alcatraz"

19. "Kitty Foyle" and "The Great Ziegfeld"

20. "Julie" and "Doctor Dolittle"

(answers on page 130)

Amnesia Victims

Column #1, below, lists eight actors who played amnesia victims involved in various murder plots. Column #2 lists, in scrambled order, the actresses who played their loyal helpmates. Column #3 lists, in scrambled order, the films in which each pair appeared. How many of these men, women and titles can you match correctly?

Column #1

1. Walter Abel
2. Warner Baxter
3. Ralph Bellamy
4. Tom Conway
5. John Hodiak
6. Pat O'Brien
7. Gregory Peck
8. William Powell

Column #2

Nancy Guild
Ingrid Bergman
Margot Grahame
Claire Trevor
Hedy Lamarr
Margaret Lindsay
Ann Rutherford
Marian Marsh

Column #3

"Crossroads"
"The Man Who Lived Twice"
"Crack-Up"
"Crime Doctor"
"Spellbound"
"Two in the Dark"
"Somewhere in the Night"
"Two O'Clock Courage"

(answers on page 130)

In the late thirties, MGM presented a series of three light-hearted mysteries in the "Thin Man" vein, all dealing with the adventures of Joel Sloane, a rare-book dealer, and his wife, Garda. A different set of performers played the Sloanes in each picture.

Listed below are the titles of the three films and the names of the six performers involved. Your job is to match the co-stars correctly, along with the title of the film in which each pair appeared.

Column #1

"Fast and Loose"
"Fast and Furious"
"Fast Company"

Column #2

Robert Montgomery
Ann Sothern
Franchot Tone
Florence Rice
Rosalind Russell
Melvyn Douglas

(answers on page 130)

 Ella Raines is watching something scary, and Franchot Tone is watching Ella, in a scene from "Phantom Lady." This film maintains its suspense even though the killer's identity is revealed the moment he appears, midway through the story. Who played the title role? (answer on page 135)

Match The Killer With The Movie

Most of these killers were "nice guys" until they were exposed in the final reel. Some masqueraded as the hero's best friend...some were businessmen who did a little murder on the side...others were phony detectives, lawyers or doctors. (We'll even tip you that one of them was a dentist!) See how many you can match with the movies in which they did their foul deeds.

1. Robert Armstrong
2. Ralph Bellamy
3. Reginald Denny
4. Douglass Dumbrille
5. Neil Hamilton
6. Sir Cedric Hardwicke
7. Victor Jory
8. Paul Lukas
9. Herbert Marshall
10. Grant Mitchell
11. Douglass Montgomery
12. Ralph Morgan
13. Chester Morris
14. Alan Mowbray
15. Conrad Nagel
16. Henry O'Neill
17. George E. Stone
18. Lyle Talbot
19. Franchot Tone
20. Donald Woods

(a) "Return of the Terror"
(b) "Thirteen Ghosts"
(c) "Experiment Perilous"
(d) "Murder in Trinidad"
(e) "The Unseen"
(f) "The Ex-Mrs. Bradford"
(g) "Phantom Lady"
(h) "One New York Night"
(i) "The Princess Comes Across"
(j) "Fog" (1934)
(k) "The Case Against Mrs. Ames"
(l) "Lured"
(m) "Footsteps in the Dark"
(n) "The Cat Creeps" (1930)
(o) "The Spider" (1931)
(p) "Transatlantic Merry-Go-Round"
(q) "The Bat Whispers"
(r) "The Second Woman"
(s) "Penguin Pool Murder"
(t) "The Cat and the Canary" (1939)

(answers on page 130)

26

In the center of this controversy is Richard Roundtree as John Shaft, a hard-hitting, fast-living Harlem detective who tangles with organized crime and the law while hunting a killer. Here, Shaft warns policeman Dan Hannafin (left) against mistreating teenager Melvin Green, Jr. From which entry in the "Shaft" series is this scene? (answer on page 135)

Match The Detective With The Movie

The movie detective has many alternate names — names like "gumshoe," "flatfoot," and "fuzz." But however unflattering his "moniker," the fact remains that no murder mystery is complete with-

out him — even if someone else solves the crime! See if you can match these twenty with the movies in which they applied their various techniques.

1. Edward Arnold
2. Ralph Bellamy
3. Charles Bickford
4. William Boyd
5. George Brent
6. Lee J. Cobb
7. Preston Foster
8. Gene Hackman
9. Jack Holt
10. Charles Laughton
11. Edmund Lowe
12. Victor McLaglen
13. Thomas Mitchell
14. Ricardo Montalban
15. Sidney Poitier
16. William Powell
17. Richard Roundtree
18. C. Aubrey Smith
19. H. B. Warner
20. George Zucco

(a) "In the Heat of the Night"
(b) "Private Detective 62"
(c) "A Dangerous Affair"
(d) "Mad Holiday"
(e) "Mystery Street"
(f) "The Menace"
(g) "The Dark Mirror"
(h) "The Firebird"
(i) "From Headquarters"
(j) "Bermuda Mystery"
(k) "London By Night"
(l) "Shaft"
(m) "The Man on the Eiffel Tower"
(n) "Remember Last Night?"
(o) "Before Midnight"
(p) "Whirlpool" (1950)
(q) "The Great Hotel Murder"
(r) "Gorilla At Large"
(s) "Night Moves"
(t) "Murder By the Clock"

(answers on page 131)

27 Detective Thomas Mitchell doesn't know whether he's confronting Olivia de Havilland or her twin sister (also played by Olivia de Havilland). All he knows is that one of them committed a murder. In what movie does this scene occur? (answer on page 135)

 28 Charles Laughton bumps off his first wife and a black-mailer in order to find happiness with his second wife, Ella Raines. Unfortunately for him, Scotland Yard steps in before he can sail away with her to Canada. Name this 1945 movie. (answer on page 135)

Unpopular Dames Who Got Rubbed Out

Each of these ladies was eliminated during the early reels of her respective movie — and if you think no one had reason for wanting them out of the way, you're dead wrong!

Let's see how right you are in matching them with the films in which they appeared (and shortly afterward **disappeared**)!

1. Evelyn Brent
2. Dorothy Burgess
3. Doris Dowling
4. Patricia Dane
5. Sonia Dresdel
6. Ava Gardner
7. Wynne Gibson
8. Rita Hayworth
9. Louise Henry
10. Rosalind Ivan
11. Rita Johnson
12. Anita Louise
13. Mayo Methot
14. Karen Morley
15. Greta Nissen

(a) "Grand Central Murder"
(b) "The Circus Queen Murder"
(c) "The Phantom of Crestwood"
(d) "The Big Clock"
(e) "The Suspect"
(f) "The Night Club Lady"
(g) "Hat, Coat and Glove"
(h) "The Blue Dahlia"
(i) "Nine Girls"
(j) "East Side, West Side"
(k) "Who Killed Gail Preston?"
(l) "Crime of the Century" (1933)
(m) "The Fallen Idol"
(n) "Attorney for the Defense"
(o) "The Casino Murder Case"

(answers on page 131)

29 Deanna Durbin, who has witnessed a murder from a train window, becomes romantically interested in one of the suspects, David Bruce. What was the name of this movie?
(answer on page 135)

Murder, Mystery & Intrigue Involving Trains

Name practically any crime — and you'll find it's been committed on a train! Movie victims have been shot, stabbed, strangled, poisoned, bitten by snakes, terrorized by time bombs, hypnotized into committing suicide and even **electrocuted** on trains! Murders have been planned on trains and witnessed from train windows. Passengers have disappeared on trains. Smugglers, forgers, jewel thieves and embezzlers have all sought getaways on trains. And justice has been served by many a killer's leap to a well-deserved death from a speeding train.

There have been trains from Paris to Berlin, Calcutta to Bombay, Istanbul to Calais, London to Edinburgh, New York to Mexico — to name just a few.

But don't worry about who did what to whom on which train. Simply match each of the following film titles with each of the casts listed below.

Titles

1. "Across the Bridge"
2. "Berlin Express"
3. "Background to Danger"
4. "Bombay Mail"
5. "Double Indemnity"
6. "I Am a Thief"
7. "Lady on a Train"
8. "The Lady Vanishes"
9. "Murder in the Private Car"
10. "Murder on the Orient Express"
11. "Orient Express"
12. "Paris Express"
13. "Peking Express"
14. "Rome Express"
15. "The Seven-Per-Cent Solution"
16. "Shadow of a Doubt"
17. "Shanghai Express"
18. "Silk Express"
19. "Strangers on a Train"
20. "Subway Express"
21. "Terror by Night"
22. "Terror on a Train"
23. "Thirteen Women"

Casts

(a) Michael Redgrave, Margaret Lockwood, Paul Lukas, Dame May Whitty, Cecil Parker, Basil Radford, Naughton Wayne

(b) Neil Hamilton, Sheila Terry, Guy Kibbee, Dudley Digges, Arthur Byron, Allen Jenkins, Harold Huber

(c) Heather Angel, Norman Foster, Ralph Morgan, Herbert Mundin, Una O'Connor, Irene Ware, Dorothy Burgess

(d) Albert Finney, Lauren Bacall, Ingrid Bergman, Sean Connery, Vanessa Redgrave, Richard Widmark, Anthony Perkins

(e) Deanna Durbin, Ralph Bellamy, Edward Everett Horton, Dan Duryea, Patrica Morison, Allen Jenkins, George Coulouris

(f) Rod Steiger, David Knight, Maria Landi, Noel Willman, Bernard Lee

(g) Esther Ralston, Conrad Veidt, Sir Cedric Hardwicke, Hugh Williams, Finlay Currie, Frank Vosper

(h) Mary Astor, Ricardo Cortez, Dudley Digges, Robert Barrat, Irving Pichel, Hobart Cavanaugh

(i) Merle Oberon, Robert Ryan, Charles Korvin, Paul Lukas, Robert Coote, Reinhold Schunzel, Fritz Kortner

(j) Marlene Dietrich, Clive Brook, Anna May Wong, Warner Oland, Eugene Pallette, Lawrence Grant, Gustav von Seyffertitz

(k) Joseph Cotten, Corinne Calvet, Edmund Gwenn, Marvin Miller, Benson Fong, Soo Yong

(l) Jack Holt, Aileen Pringle, Fred Kelsey, Alan Roscoe, Jason Robards Sr., Sidney Bracy

(m) Charlie Ruggles, Una Merkel, Mary Carlisle, Russell Hardie, Porter Hall, Willard Robertson

(n) Fred MacMurray, Barbara Stanwyck, Edward G. Robinson, Porter Hall, Jean Heather, Tom Powers, Byron Barr

(o) Basil Rathbone, Nigel Bruce, Alan Mowbray, Dennis Hoey, Billy Bevan, Mary Forbes, Renee Godfrey

(p) Farley Granger, Ruth Roman, Robert Walker, Leo G. Carroll, Patricia Hitchcock, Laura Elliott, Marion Lorne

(q) Irene Dunne, Ricardo Cortez, Myrna Loy, Kay Johnson, Florence Eldridge, Jill Esmond, C. Henry Gordon

(r) Edmund Lowe, Shirley Grey, Onslow Stevens, Ralph Forbes, Hedda Hopper, John Davidson

(s) George Raft, Brenda Marshall, Sydney Greenstreet, Peter Lorre, Osa Massen, Kurt Katch, Turhan Bey

(t) Glenn Ford, Anne Vernon, Harcourt Williams, Victor Maddern, Harold Warrender, Bill Fraser

(u) Nicol Williamson, Alan Arkin, Vanessa Redgrave, Robert Duvall, Laurence Olivier, Joel Grey, Samantha Eggar

(v) Claude Rains, Marta Toren, Marius Goring, Herbert Lom, Felix Aylmer, Anouk

(w) Joseph Cotten, Teresa Wright, Macdonald Carey, Patricia Collinge, Hume Cronyn, Henry Travers, Wallace Ford

(answers on page 131)

Murder Mysteries About Movies & Movie Stars

Does this plot sound familiar? A movie star receives an anonymous note threatening his life. While filming a scene from his latest picture, he suddenly falls to the floor, dead. Somebody, it seems, had put real bullets in the gun that was used in the scene where he was supposed to be shot.

Whodunit? Was it his jealous wife? His cast-off mistress? His blackmailing valet? Or was it the stand-in who did all the dirty work while the star took all the credit?

Well, maybe you've never seen **exactly** that same plot before. But chances are you've enjoyed many similar murder mysteries with Hollywood backgrounds. Here are some typical examples. See how many casts and titles you can match correctly.

Titles

1. "The Death Kiss"
2. "The Falcon in Hollywood"
3. "Fugitives for a Night"   4. "The Hollywood Story"
5. "In a Lonely Place"   6. "The Last of Sheila"
7. "The Preview Murder Mystery"
8. "The Studio Murder Mystery"   9. "Super-Sleuth"
10. "What Ever Happened to Baby Jane?"
11. "The Whole Truth"

Casts

(a) Reginald Denny, Frances Drake, Gail Patrick, Rod La Rocque, Ian Keith, George Barbier, Conway Tearle

(b) Stewart Granger, Donna Reed, George Sanders, Gianna Maria Canale

(c) Neil Hamilton, Doris Hill, Fredric March, Warner Oland, Florence Eldridge, Eugene Pallette, Chester Conklin

(d) Bette Davis, Joan Crawford, Victor Buono, Marjorie Bennett, Maidie Norman, Anna Lee, Barbara Merrill

(e) David Manners, Adrienne Ames, Bela Lugosi, John Wray, Vince Barnett, Alexander Carr, Edward Van Sloan

(f) Frank Albertson, Eleanor Lynn, Allan Lane, Bradley Page, Adrienne Ames, Jonathan Hale, Russell Hicks.

(g) Tom Conway, Barbara Hale, Veda Ann Borg, John Abbott, Sheldon Leonard, Konstantin Shayne, Emory Parnell

(h) Humphrey Bogart, Gloria Grahame, Frank Lovejoy, Carl Benton Reid, Art Smith, Jeff Donnell, Martha Stewart

(i) James Mason, Raquel Welch, James Coburn, Dyan Cannon, Richard Benjamin, Ian McShane, Joan Hackett

(j) Richard Conte, Julie Adams, Richard Egan, Henry Hull, Fred Clark, Jim Backus, Houseley Stevenson

(k) Jack Oakie, Ann Sothern, Eduardo Ciannelli, Alan Bruce, Edgar Kennedy, Joan Woodbury, Bradley Page

(answers on page 131)

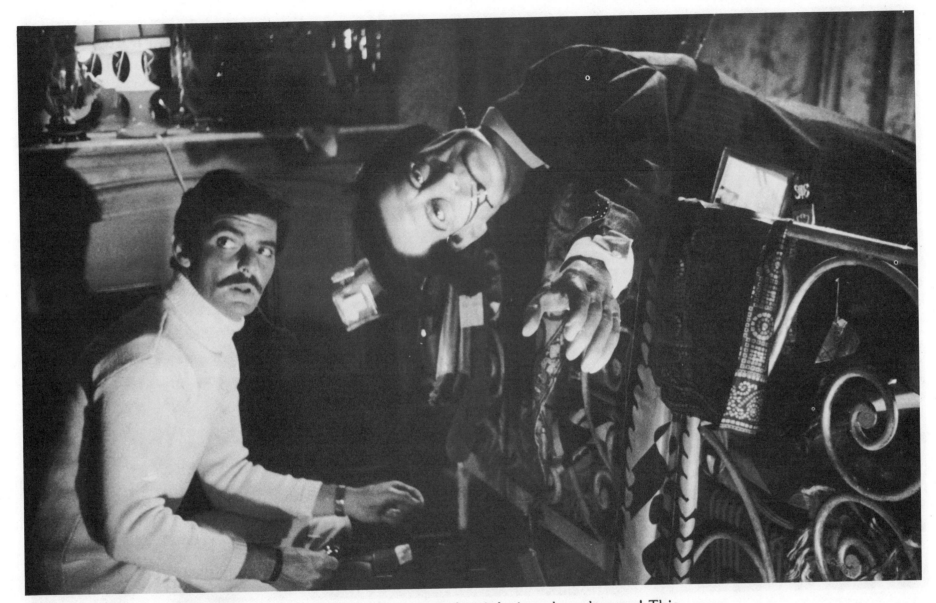

30 Don't faint — the one on the right is only a dummy! This scene is from "The Last of Sheila." The story deals with a producer who invites six movie people on his yacht to learn which one killed his wife. Strange games are played to uncover the guilty party. Who's the actor on the left? (answer on page 135)

 In this 1946 mystery, George Raft played a hard-boiled Hollywood detective investigating the murder of a famous composer. The film was produced by Joan Harrison, who began her career with the master, Alfred Hitchcock. Do you know the title? (answer on page 135)

Each of the following plots describes a murder mystery in which music in one form or another played a key role. How many can you identify?

1. While the unsuspecting audience out front enjoys an elaborate Earl Carroll musical revue, two women (Gail Patrick and Gertrude Michael) are murdered backstage.

2. Refusing to accept the death of a philandering Hollywood songwriter (Edward Ashley) as suicide, a stubborn detective (George Raft) seeks the killer from among the deceased's legion of female friends (Lynn Bari, Virginia Huston, Myrna Dell, et al.), many of whom have weak alibis.

3. Schoolteacher Hildegarde Withers (Edna May Oliver) discovers the identity of a killer by deciphering a couple of lines of music that have been written in chalk on a classroom blackboard.

4. Leo Carrillo, a tenor in an opera company singing nightly at the Hollywood Bowl, is murdered in full view of 20,000 spectators.

5. Pirouetting gracefully before the footlights as the star of an ice-skating revue, Vera Hruba Ralston becomes a prime suspect in the murder of a theatrical impresario who had blackmailed several former lady friends.

6. A ruthless radio crooner (Arnold Gray) is murdered but not mourned when it is discovered that a "ghost" had done his singing for him. The "crooner" had merely synchronized his lips to the words, which were actually sung by his crippled piano accompanist (Ralph Forbes) behind the scenes.

7. While a scantily clad Barbara Stanwyck entertains the paying customers in a burlesque house with some snappy song-and-dance numbers, a mad killer turns the backstage area of the theatre into an arena of terror.

(answers on page 131)

 Police inspector Alastair Sim (left) is intrigued by the bitter rivalry that exists between doctors Trevor Howard (center) and Leo Genn, both of whom are under suspicion for murder. Name the movie. (answer on page 135)

Each of the following plot skeletons describes a murder mystery in which color is part of the title. The film's cast appears in parenthesis after the description. Give the title of each movie.

1. After a rich old woman on her deathbed miraculously recovers, she is murdered by a member of her greedy household. The reading of her will is interrupted by the arrival of a real-estate promoter and an antique dealer. (Basil Rathbone, Hugh Herbert, Broderick Crawford, Bela Lugosi, Gale Sondergaard, Alan Ladd)

2. A World War II veteran, freshly out of the service, becomes a prime suspect when his faithless wife is found slain in her bungalow. (Alan Ladd, Veronica Lake, William Bendix, Howard da Silva, Doris Dowling, Tom Powers)

3. A girl flees after hitting a drunk over the head with a poker while defending her honor. Believing she has slain her attacker, she confides her secret to a newspaperman who finds the real killer. (Anne Baxter, Richard Conte, Ann Sothern, Raymond Burr, Jeff Donnell)

4. A discharged secret-service agent, reduced to cataloging butterflies, aids a young girl falsely accused of murder. (Jean Simmons, Trevor Howard, Sonia Dresdel, Barry Jones, Kenneth More)

5. A droll Scotland Yard inspector investigates a series of bizarre murders that occur in a British hospital between buzz-bomb attacks during World War II. (Sally Gray, Trevor Howard, Leo Genn, Alastair Sim, Rosamund John)

6. A deaf mute accused of an apparently motiveless crime is defended in court by a flamboyant French attorney. (Michael Redgrave, Kieron Moore, Ann Todd, Leo Genn, Jane Griffiths)

7. A farmer and his sister share a horrible secret concerning a sinister house in the woods. (Edward G. Robinson, Lon McAllister, Judith Anderson, Allene Roberts, Rory Calhoun, Julie London)

8. Many years after several mysterious deaths in an allegedly haunted room of a castle, a beautiful girl's three suitors decide that each will spend a night alone in the room, to debunk the legend. (Lionel Atwill, Gloria Stuart, Paul Lukas, Edward Arnold, Onslow Stevens, William Janney)

9. Mystery and murder at a French chateâu surround an American girl whose only proof of claim to a fortune is a vital scrap of paper. (Jean Muir, Ricardo Cortez, Ruth Donnelly, Minna Gombell, Walter Kingsford, John Eldredge)

10. An evil count plots to kill twin sisters and acquire their fortune by first driving them insane. (Alexis Smith, Eleanor Parker, Sydney Greenstreet, Gig Young, Agnes Moorehead, John Abbott)

(answers on page 132)

33 This murder mystery was done in the "Thin Man" style. William Powell as a surgeon co-starred with Jean Arthur as his ex-wife, a mystery story writer who fancies herself a sleuth. Together they solve a baffling series of murders. Do you know the title of this film? (answer on page 135)

Creative Homicides

The homicides described below are not the everyday kind. They're so unconventional, in fact, that they rate being singled out for sheer originality! Can you identify the movies in which these elaborate killings took place? The principal cast members of each film are included, to make it easier for you.

1. A chef is roasted in his own oven. (George Segal, Jacqueline Bisset, Robert Morley)

2. A zoologist avenges himself on his wife's seducer by sewing the victim's lips together and leaving him to perish in the jungle. (Lionel Atwill, Charlie Ruggles, Gail Patrick, Randolph Scott)

3. A philandering husband lures his wife into a department store...kills her with a bow and arrow...and plants her body in the window as part of a drawing-room display, where it makes a convenient fourth at bridge. (Lew Ayres, June Knight, Alice White, Eugene Pallette, Alan Dinehart, Minna Gombell)

4. A one-armed scientist uses a hand made of synthetic flesh to strangle female victims. (Lionel Atwill, Fay Wray, Lee Tracy, Preston Foster)

5. A jockey is fatally bitten during a horse race by means of a gelatin capsule containing a black widow spider which was planted on him before the race. (William Powell, Jean Arthur, James Gleason, Eric Blore, Robert Armstrong)

(answers on page 132)

 Charles Boyer and Jessica Tandy in a scene from a murder mystery that was written for the screen by Aldous Huxley from his short story, **The Gioconda Smile**. What was the film's title? (answer on page 135)

Here are the names of eight actors. Below them is a list of eight roles, one of which was played by each actor. Following this list are the various films in which each actor played the role described. Your job is to match each player, part and picture correctly.

Players

1. Charles Boyer
2. Montgomery Clift
3. Gary Cooper
4. Paul Lukas
5. William Powell
6. Claude Rains
7. Lewis Stone
8. Spencer Tracy

Parts

(a) A radio commentator specializing in crime tales, who turns fiction into reality.

(b) A novelist who gets murdered — and the suspects are all married women whom he once romanced and then described in his books.

(c) A philandering playboy who is put on trial for poisoning his wife.

(d) An actor who keeps confessing to murders he didn't commit, in hopes that he won't be believed when he finally confesses to the crime he really intends to commit.

(e) A crime reporter who, while investigating a murder, reveals himself to be the killer.

(f) A brain surgeon who tries to learn why a wealthy dowager insists that her niece is insane and in need of a lobotomy.

(g) A lawyer who is accused of murder when a gossip columnist is shot dead in his apartment.

(h) An American businessman in London who is suspected by his wife of being a murderer on the loose.

Pictures

"The Man Who Cried Wolf"

"Star of Midnight"   "Murder Man"

"The Unsuspected"   "The Naked Edge"

"Suddenly, Last Summer"

"Affairs of a Gentleman"

"A Woman's Vengeance"

(answers on page 132)

35 Here, Dana Andrews is romancing Alice Faye, but his mind is really on Linda Darnell, who is later murdered. Who played the killer, and what was this film's title? (answer on page 135)

Cast Out The Non-Cast Member

Pick out the one player who was **not** in the cast of each of the following films:

1. "The Big Fix" — Richard Dreyfuss, Susan Anspach, Bonnie Bedelia, John Lithgow, Fritz Weaver, Murray Hamilton

2. "A Blueprint for Murder" — Joseph Cotten, Jean Peters, Gary Merrill, Catherine McLeod, Jack Kruschen, Rhys Williams

3. "Charade" — Cary Grant, Audrey Hepburn, Walter Matthau, James Coburn, George Kennedy, Walter Abel, Ned Glass

4. "The Cheap Detective" — Peter Falk, Peter Sellers, Louise Fletcher, Marsha Mason, Madeline Kahn, Dom DeLuise, Sid Caesar

5. "Chinatown" — Jack Nicholson, Faye Dunaway, John Huston, Ann-Margret, Roman Polanski, Diane Ladd

6. "The Dark Mirror" — Olivia de Havilland, Lew Ayres, Thomas Mitchell, Victor Jory, Richard Long, Garry Owen

7. "Death on the Nile" — Bette Davis, Peter Ustinov, David Niven, Angela Lansbury, Janet Leigh, Mia Farrow, Maggie Smith

8. "The Drowning Pool" — Paul Newman, Joanne Woodward, Tony Franciosa, Lee Remick, Murray Hamilton

9. "Fallen Angel" — Alice Faye, Dana Andrews, George Sanders, Linda Darnell, Charles Bickford, Bruce Cabot

10. "Foul Play" — Goldie Hawn, Chevy Chase, Burgess Meredith, Karen Black, Dudley Moore, Rachel Roberts

11. "Games" — Simone Signoret, James Caan, Katharine Ross, William Devane, Kent Smith, Estelle Winwood

12. "Harper" — Paul Newman, Lauren Bacall, Julie Andrews, Janet Leigh, Shelley Winters, Robert Wagner

13. "Klute" — Jane Fonda, Donald Sutherland, Roy Scheider, Charles Cioffi, Dorothy Tristan, Shelley Duvall

14. "Laura" — Gene Tierney, Dana Andrews, Clifton Webb, Vincent Price, Judith Anderson, June Havoc

15. "The Long Goodbye" — Elliott Gould, Nina van Pallandt, Bruce Dern, Sterling Hayden, Mark Rydell, Henry Gibson

16. "The Mad Miss Manton" — Henry Fonda, Barbara Stanwyck, Gail Patrick, Sam Levene, Penny Singleton, Stanley Ridges

17. "Marlowe" — James Garner, Gayle Hunnicutt, Carroll O'Connor, Rita Moreno, Roy Scheider, Jackie Coogan

18. "Mirage" — Gregory Peck, Diane Baker, Walter Matthau, Gene Hackman, Walter Abel, George Kennedy, Jack Weston

19. "Murder By Death" — Peter Falk, Alec Guinness, Peter Sellers, David Niven, Maggie Smith, Angela Lansbury, Truman Capote

20. "Remains To Be Seen" — June Allyson, Van Johnson, Gloria DeHaven, Angela Lansbury, Louis Calhern, Dorothy Dandridge

21. "Scream of Fear" — Susan Strasberg, Ronald Lewis, Ann Todd, Peter Cushing, Christopher Lee

22. "Woman of Straw" — Gina Lollobrigida, Sean Connery, Ralph Richardson, Alexander Knox, Herbert Lom

(answers on page 133)

36 Scientist Van Heflin, police captain Cliff Clark, and lab assistant Marsha Hunt take a breather in "Kid Glove Killer." In this unusual whodunit, the killer is discovered by means of tiny bits of evidence seen through the police-laboratory microscope. The director of this 1942 film won Oscars in 1953 and 1966. What's his name? (answer on page 135)

From the cast of each of the following films, select the actor or actress who played the killer:

1. "Above Suspicion" — Joan Crawford, Fred MacMurray, Conrad Veidt, Basil Rathbone, Reginald Owen, Richard Ainley, Ann Shoemaker

2. "Beyond a Reasonable Doubt" — Dana Andrews, Joan Fontaine, Sidney Blackmer, Philip Bourneuf, Shepperd Strudwick, Arthur Franz, Edward Binns

3. "Crack-Up" — Pat O'Brien, Claire Trevor, Herbert Marshall, Ray Collins, Wallace Ford, Dean Harens, Erskine Sanford

4. "Crime of the Century" — Jean Hersholt, Wynne Gibson, Stuart Erwin, Frances Dee, David Landau, Robert Elliott, Gordon Westcott

5. "Crossfire" — Robert Young, Robert Mitchum, Robert Ryan, Gloria Grahame, Paul Kelly, Sam Levene, Jacqueline White

6. "Death on the Diamond" — Robert Young, Madge Evans, Ted Healy, Nat Pendleton, Paul Kelly, DeWitt Jennings, Mickey Rooney

7. "Fingers at the Window" — Lew Ayres, Laraine Day, Basil Rathbone, Walter Kingsford, Miles Mander, Charles D. Brown, Cliff Clark

8. "Grand Central Murder" — Van Heflin, Patricia Dane, Sam Levene, Cecilia Parker, Virginia Grey, Tom Conway, Samuel S. Hinds

9. "Kid Glove Killer" — Van Heflin, Marsha Hunt, Lee Bowman, Samuel S. Hinds, Cliff Clark, Eddie Quillan, John Litel

10. "Lady in the Lake" — Robert Montgomery, Audrey Totter, Lloyd Nolan, Tom Tully, Leon Ames, Jayne Meadows, Dick Simmons

11. "Midnight Lace" — Doris Day, Rex Harrison, John Gavin, Myrna Loy, Herbert Marshall, Roddy McDowall, John Williams

12. "Moss Rose" — Peggy Cummins, Victor Mature, Ethel Barrymore, Vincent Price, George Zucco, Patricia Medina, Rhys Williams

13. "Murder in the Fleet" — Robert Taylor, Jean Parker, Ted Healy, Una Merkel, Nat Pendleton, Jean Hersholt, Donald Cook

14. "Murder She Said" — Margaret Rutherford, Arthur Kennedy, Muriel Pavlov, James Robertson Justice, Ronald Howard, Charles Tingwell, Stringer Davis

15. "Nine Girls" — Ann Harding, Evelyn Keyes, Jinx Falkenburg, Anita Louise, Leslie Brooks, Nina Foch, William Demarest

16. "The Phantom of Crestwood" — Ricardo Cortez, Karen Morley, H. B. Warner, Pauline Frederick, Anita Louise, Sam Hardy, Skeets Gallagher

17. "The Sleeping City" — Richard Conte, Coleen Gray, Richard Taber, John Alexander, Peggy Dow, Alex Nicol

18. "Somewhere in the Night" — John Hodiak, Nancy Guild, Richard Conte, Lloyd Nolan, Josephine Hutchinson, Fritz Kortner, Sheldon Leonard

37 "Lady in the Lake" was a whodunit told in the first person. The entire action was shown through the eyes of the central character played by Robert Montgomery (left). Here, Mr. Montgomery, who was also the director, discusses a scene with players Leon Ames and Audrey Totter. Who wrote the original story on which this film was based? (answer on page 135)

19. "The Spiral Staircase" — Dorothy McGuire, George Brent, Ethel Barrymore, Kent Smith, Elsa Lanchester, Rhonda Fleming, Gordon Oliver

20. "Strait-Jacket" — Joan Crawford, Diane Baker, Leif Erickson, George Kennedy, Howard St. John, Rochelle Hudson, Edith Atwater

21. "Tomorrow at Seven" — Chester Morris, Vivienne Osborne, Frank McHugh, Allen Jenkins, Henry Stephenson, Oscar Apfel, Grant Mitchell

22. "Witness for the Prosecution" — Tyrone Power, Marlene Dietrich, Charles Laughton, Elsa Lanchester, Henry Daniell, John Williams, Una O'Connor

23. "Woman on the Run" — Ann Sheridan, Dennis O'Keefe, Robert Keith, Ross Elliott, Frank Jenks, J. Farrell MacDonald, Steven Geray

(answers on page 133)

Nostalgia Potpourri

 Edward Arnold and Rosemary De Camp in a scene from a 1942 thriller, in which he played a blind detective. The film's suspense did not derive from the plot itself, but rather from the audience's instinctive sense of this man's helplessness in tight situations. Can you name the movie? (answer on page 135)

Here's a grab bag of questions that require you to dip into your memory bank of movie titles. How many of these "oldies" can you name?

1. What 1936 movie was based on an idea by President Franklin D. Roosevelt? The leads were played by Henry Wilcoxon, Betty Furness, Sidney Blackmer and Evelyn Brent.

2. Name the 1945 movie in which Edward Arnold played a blind detective named Duncan MacLain.

3. A crime-solving nun (Claudette Colbert) saves a wrongly convicted girl (Ann Blyth) from being hanged. Name this 1951 movie.

4. Name the two movies (1932 and 1933) in which the debonair Adolphe Menjou played detective Thatcher Colt.

5. A gambler (John Halliday) with hypnotic powers accidentally mesmerizes a young man (Tom Brown) who commits murder while in a trance. Name this 1934 film. Sir Guy Standing and Judith Allen were also in the cast.

6. Jeanne Crain played a distraught bride whose husband (Carl Betz) mysteriously disappears during their honeymoon aboard a transatlantic ocean liner. Name this 1953 movie.

7. Name the 1932 movie in which football player John Mack Brown was murdered while running down the field to make a touchdown in full view of 70,000 spectators. Phillips Holmes, Dorothy Jordan and Charlie Ruggles had prominent roles.

8. A deranged husband (Robert Montgomery), believing that his best friend (George Sanders) is having an affair with his wife (Ingrid Bergman), kills himself in a manner that throws suspicion on the friend. At the eleventh hour, the friend is saved by the disclosure of the dead man's diary. Name this 1941 film.

9. In what 1932 film was defendant Joan Bennett, on trial for murder, defended by attorney Donald Cook? Skeets Gallagher and ZaSu Pitts played court reporters.

10. An artist (Alan Ladd), accused of murdering his alcoholic wife (Carolyn Jones), produces a tape recording that leads to the discovery of the real killer. Name this 1959 movie.

11. The morning after an orgy, during which one of the merrymakers was murdered, none of the participants can recall what happened because they were all drunk. Based on a novel called **The Hangover Murders**, this 1935 film featured Robert Young and Constance Cummings as the ringleaders of the chipper crowd. Name the movie.

12. Name the 1933 film in which the murderer makes a practice of presenting each of his victims with an ace of spades, on which appears the hour of his intended arrival. Chester Morris starred, with Frank McHugh and Allen Jenkins featured as a pair of comic detectives.

13. What 1936 movie dealt with murder in a department store? Robert Young, Florence Rice and Ted Healy played the leads.

14. The name of a beautiful girl who is murdered provided the title for an unusual British murder mystery with racial overtones. The leading role in this 1959 film was played by Nigel Patrick as the superintendent of police investigating the crime. What's the title?

15. In a 1934 film, a criminologist (Otto Kruger), whose wife (Karen Morley) is having an affair with an author (Nils Asther), plans and executes a "perfect murder," which he pins on the author. This film had the same title as a 1943 film which was the first in a series that starred Warner Baxter. Except for the title, the two films were totally dissimilar. Give the title.

16. Name the 1942 Bud Abbott-Lou Costello movie in which the boys played a pair of aspiring radio writers who become involved in murder at a broadcasting studio. William Bendix had the role of a flustered detective.

(answers on page 133)

39 Physician Michael Rennie is threatened by a rash of poison-pen letters when he takes up practice in a Quebec community. Here, he is visited by town siren Linda Darnell who is infatuated with him. Name the movie.
(answer on page 135)

Match The Co-Stars With The Title

Column #1 below lists the male and female leads of twenty films. Column #2 lists the films in which each pair appeared. See how many couples and titles you can match correctly.

Column #1

1. Gracie Allen & William Post Jr.
2. Heather Angel & Nigel Bruce
3. Mary Astor & Edward G. Robinson
4. Joan Bennett & Edmund Lowe
5. Joan Blondell & Tom Brown
6. Nancy Carroll & Cary Grant
7. Claudette Colbert & Robert Ryan
8. Linda Darnell & Charles Boyer
9. Bette Davis & Donald Woods
10. Ellen Drew & Robert Preston
11. Ann Dvorak & Lyle Talbot
12. Glenda Farrell & Ben Lyon
13. Kay Francis & Lionel Barrymore
14. Ann Harding & Walter Abel
15. Margaret Lindsay & Bruce Cabot
16. Carole Lombard & Randolph Scott
17. Merle Oberon & Franchot Tone
18. Ann Sheridan & Patric Knowles
19. Ann Sothern & Edmund Lowe
20. Loretta Young & Franchot Tone

Column #2

(a) "The Woman Accused"
(b) "Dark Waters"
(c) "Girl Missing"
(d) "The Witness Chair"
(e) "Sinner Take All"
(f) "Supernatural"
(g) "Scotland Yard" (1930)
(h) "The Famous Ferguson Case"
(i) "Guilty Hands"
(j) "The Thirteenth Letter"
(k) "The Unguarded Hour"
(l) "The Man with Two Faces"
(m) "Fog Over Frisco"
(n) "Grand Exit"
(o) "The Patient in Room 18"
(p) "The Night of January 16th"
(q) "Murder in Trinidad"
(r) "The Secret Fury"
(s) "Mr. and Mrs. North"
(t) "Murder in the Clouds"

(answers on page 133)

40 Susan Hayward casts a dubious glance at Bill Williams, a sailor on leave, who has six hours to prove that he didn't commit a murder. The film is titled, appropriately enough, "Deadline at Dawn." Who played the killer?
(answer on page 135)

Guess the identity of these players from their real names plus an added clue or two. (Real names are in bold face.)

1. **Leslie Townes Hope** and **Pauline Levy** co-starred in two comedy murder mysteries, one of which was "The Ghost Breakers." Name the other one, and give the screen names of these two players.

2. His real name was **Etienne Pelissier Jacques de Bujac**. He played the killer in "Murder on the Blackboard" and a suspect in "Fallen Angel." He was once married to Adrienne Ames. By what screen name was he known?

3. This handsome leading man of the thirties played in "Dracula," "The Mystery of Edwin Drood," "The Death Kiss," "Moonstone" and the 1934 version of "The Black Cat." His real name is **Rauff de Ryther Duan Acklom**. What's his screen name?

4. **Ann McKim** had important roles in "Murder in the Clouds," "The Case of the Stuttering Bishop" and "Stronger than Desire." She once played Paul Muni's sister. What's her movie name?

5. You've seen **Raymond Guion** in "Seven Keys to Baldpate" (1935 version), "The Night of June 13th" and "Transatlantic Merry-Go-Round." He was married to a very famous singing star of the movies. What name would he use on a movie theatre marquee?

6. **Jeannette Helen Morrison** played the biggest scene of her career in a shower. What's her screen name, and what's the movie?

7. **William Joseph Shields** played a murderous judge in an Agatha Christie classic. What was his screen name, and what's the name of the film?

8. **Violet Mary Klotz** was a murder victim in "Penthouse" (1933) and a suspect in "Penguin Pool Murder," but she's best known for appearing in a scene from a famous gangster movie involving a grapefruit. What's her screen name?

9. **Thomas Charles Sanders** played in "Grand Central Murder," "The Trial of Mary Dugan" (1941 version) and "The Cat People." He also played a famous sleuth ten times on the screen, and had an even more famous brother. By what name was he known in films?

10. **Helen Marie Jurgens** starred in "The Cat Creeps" (1930) and "The Spanish Cape Mystery." She was sometimes facetiously referred to as Rin-Tin-Tin's favorite actress. What name did she use in the movies?

11. **George Brendan Nolan** played the killer in a popular thriller involving a mute servant girl. He also figured prominently in "Miss Pinkerton," "From Headquarters" and "The Corpse Came C.O.D." What name did he use on a movie marquee?

12. You saw **Guenther Schneider** in "The Secret of the Blue Room" and "Slightly Honorable." He also played a blind detective. By what name was he known on the cast sheet?

13. This actress appeared as a suspect in "After the Thin Man" using her real name of **Dorothy McNulty**. She subsequently acted in films under a different name, and is better known as the nitwit blonde housewife of a comedy series. What screen name did she adopt for these later films?

14. You laughed at the antics of **Lewis Delaney Offield** as the "Super-Sleuth." He also played a suspect in "Murder at the Vanities." What was his movie name?

15. **Margaret Fitzpatrick** appeared in five pictures with "murder" in the title: "Murder at the Vanities," "Murder with Pictures," "Quiet Please, Murder," "Murders in the Zoo" and "The Preview Murder Mystery." What's her screen name?

16. **Emma Matzo** played bad girls in "Dead Reckoning" and "Too Late for Tears," and a good girl in "The Strange Love of Martha Ivers." By what name is she known on the cast sheet?

17. **Ernest Carlton Brimmer** starred in "Seven Keys to Baldpate" (1929 version) and "The Whistler" series. What name did he use on the screen?

18. **Melvyn Edouard Hesselberg** is among the most versatile actors on the screen, and has been a star since the early thirties. Among his films are "The Old Dark House," "Woman in the Dark" and "Tell No Tales." What name does he use in the movies?

19. **Edythe Marrener** was a Brooklyn girl who made good in a big way. You saw her in "Deadline at Dawn," "They Won't Believe Me" and "The Honey Pot." By what screen name was she known?

20. **Lucile Vasconcells Langhanke** has appeared in films involving such sleuths as Sam Spade, Perry Mason and Philo Vance. In addition, she played in "The Man with Two Faces," "The Murder of Dr. Harrigan" and "A Kiss Before Dying." What's her movie name?

(answers on page 134)

41 Ray Milland, shown here with Rita Johnson, finds himself a hunted man in this suspense melodrama. Ray's boss kills Rita and then calls upon Ray to find the killer. The clues are so cleverly rigged that Ray incriminates himself by the evidence he uncovers. What's the film's title?
(answer on page 135)

1. Which two cast members of the 1941 "Maltese Falcon" repeated their roles in the 1975 sequel, "The Black Bird"?

2. Name the 1944 Paramount movie in which Basil Rathbone and Nigel Bruce appeared together in the supporting cast, but did **not** play Sherlock Holmes and Dr. Watson. (Joan Fontaine and Arturo de Cordova had the leads.)

3. In two murder mysteries early in her career — "The Thirteenth Guest" and "A Shriek in the Night" — Ginger Rogers played opposite the same leading man. What's his name?

4. Ralph Bellamy and William Gargan, each of whom played Ellery Queen several times on the screen, appeared **together** in **two** films (**not** murder mysteries) in which they played entirely different roles. Frances Dee played the feminine lead in the first film, and Josephine Hutchinson in the second. Can you name these two films?

5. In what murder mystery did Kirk Douglas, Robert Mitchum, Tony Curtis, Frank Sinatra and Burt Lancaster all appear in cameo roles, wearing various disguises?

6. What two actors with the same last name played the same fictional detective character, and in what film did each play this role?

7. The screenplay for "Watch on the Rhine" was written by what very famous author of detective fiction? (This man was portrayed on the screen in a highly acclaimed Jane Fonda film.)

8. In 1936, RKO made a detective movie called "Muss 'em Up," in which the leading character was a private eye named Tip O'Neill. Who played this role?

9. In the supporting cast of "Frisco Kid," a 1935 James Cagney picture, there were two actors who each, shortly thereafter, took a turn at playing Perry Mason. Name these two players.

10. A 1934 film had a plot similar to Agatha Christie's **And Then There Were None** and **Ten Little Indians**: An unknown host telegraphs a dinner invitation to eight people, each of whom has a reason for killing one of the others. With the exception of the romantic leads (Donald Cook and Genevieve Tobin), all the guests are systematically eliminated, one by one. Hardie Albright played the killer. Name this film, which was based on an Owen Davis play.

11. Basil (Sherlock Holmes) Rathbone and Louis (The Saint) Hayward appeared together in the cast of a 1935 drama in which top billing went to Pauline Lord. Billie Burke and Wendy Barrie played other roles. Name the film.

12. The gimmick of stopping the action toward the climax and giving the audience a "whodunit break" — exactly one minute by the clock to review the evidence and guess the murderer — was used in the 1966 version of "Ten Little Indians." This same gimmick was used in a 1933 mystery featuring Jean Hersholt, Wynne Gibson, Stuart Erwin and Frances Dee. Can you name this earlier film?

13. George Sanders and Louis Hayward, each of whom played The Saint more than once, appeared **together** in **two** films (**not** murder mysteries) in which they played entirely different roles. Joan Bennett played the female lead in the first film, and Hedy Lamarr in the second. Name the two films.

14. Prominent in the cast of the 1934 Warner Brothers musical drama, "Wonder Bar" (top billing given to Al Jolson) were an actor who later played Philip Marlowe and an actor who later played Perry Mason. Name these two actors.

15. Name the two murder melodramas in which Charles Laughton, Ray Milland and Maureen O'Sullivan appeared together. In the first film (1932), Laughton as Maureen's father kills his nephew, Milland, in order to obtain access to the latter's money, and buries the body in his garden. In the second film (1948), Milland, a magazine editor married to Maureen, is hunted for a murder committed by Laughton, his publisher.

16. Every movie buff remembers the Hitchcock classic, "Shadow of a Doubt." But how many recall a 1935 MGM murder mystery with a slightly shorter title: "Shadow of Doubt"? Based on a story by Arthur Somers Roche, it dealt with an irrepressible dowager who comes out of a twenty-year seclusion to solve the double murder of a nasty playboy and his elderly butler. Rate yourself "A-plus" if you know who played the romantic leads.

17. A highlight of the all-star variety film, "Paramount on Parade" (1930), was a comedy skit satirizing murder mysteries. It involved Dr. Fu Manchu, Sherlock Holmes, Philo Vance and Sergeant Heath. Who played these roles in the skit?

18. During the late sixties, Frank Sinatra starred in three whodunits: "The Detective," "Tony Rome" and "Lady in Cement." His six leading ladies (two in each picture) were Jacqueline Bisset, Lainie Kazan, Lee Remick, Gena Rowlands, Jill St. John and Raquel Welch. Which two ladies appeared in each picture?

(answers on page 134)

Answers

"THE THIN MAN" SERIES

Here's the Plot — Name the Picture

1. (c)   2. (e)   3. (a)   4. (b)   5. (f)   6. (d)

Here's the Killer — Name the Picture

1. (f)   2. (b)   3. (e)   4. (c)   5. (a)   6. (d)

Here are the Victims — Name the Picture

1. (c)   2. (b)   3. (d)   4. (e)   5. (a)   6. (d)

Here are the Suspects — Name the Picture

1. (e)   2. (d)   3. (b)   4. (f)   5. (c)   6. (a)

Other "Thin Man" Questions

1. (a) & (d)   2. (c) & (e)   3. (e)   4. (b)   5. (d)   6. (e)

CHARLIE CHAN

Titles

(a) Toler   (b) Toler   (c) Winters   (d) Oland   (e) Toler   (f) Toler   (g) Winters   (h) Toler
(i) Oland   (j) Oland   (k) Winters   (l) Toler   (m) Toler

Players

1. "Charlie Chan in Egypt"   2. "Charlie Chan at the Opera"   3. "The Black Camel"   4. "Charlie Chan in London"   5. "The Black Camel"   6. "Charlie Chan Carries On"

Plots

1. "Charlie Chan at the Circus"   2. "Charlie Chan at the Opera"   3. "Charlie Chan in Egypt"   4. "The Black Camel"   5. "Charlie Chan in London"   6. "Charlie Chan at the Race Track"   7. "Charlie Chan in Shanghai"   8. "Charlie Chan on Broadway"   9. "Charlie Chan at the Olympics"   10. "Charlie Chan in Panama"

Wise Sayings

1. (g) 2. (f) 3. (a) 4. (e) 5. (d) 6. (c) 7. (b)

Other "Charlie Chan" Questions

1. "Charlie Chan's Greatest Case" 2. "Charlie Chan in Paris" 3. "Behind That Curtain" 4. Warner Baxter 5. E. L. Park

SHERLOCK HOLMES

Plots

1. "The Woman in Green" 2. "The Adventures of Sherlock Holmes" 3. "Sherlock Holmes Faces Death" 4. "Terror By Night" 5. "Sherlock Holmes in Washington" 6. "Sherlock Holmes and the Secret Weapon" 7. "The House of Fear" 8. "Spider Woman" 9. "The Pearl of Death" 10. "Pursuit to Algiers"

Other "Sherlock Holmes" Questions

1. Clive Brook — "The Return of Sherlock Holmes" 2. Dennis Hoey 3. "The Adventures of Sherlock Holmes" — Richard Greene 4. "A Study in Terror" (1965), "Murder By Decree" (1979), Frank Finlay 5. Arthur Wontner 6. "Dressed to Kill" 7. Leo McKern 8. "Sherlock Holmes" (1932) 9. Mary Gordon 10. Sir Henry Baskerville in "The Hound of the Baskervilles," Sherlock Holmes in "Sherlock Holmes and the Necklace of Death," Mycroft Holmes in "The Private Life of Sherlock Holmes" 11. "The Speckled Band" 12. Reginald Owen — Played Dr. Watson in "Sherlock Holmes," Played Sherlock Holmes in "A Study in Scarlet" 13. "They Might Be Giants" 14. Robert Stephens (Holmes) & Colin Blakely (Watson) 15. Christopher Plummer (Holmes) & James Mason (Watson) 16. Nicol Williamson (Holmes) & Robert Duvall (Watson) 17. George Zucco, Lionel Atwill, Henry Daniell 18. "The Seven-Per-Cent Solution" 19. "Sherlock Holmes" (Inspector Gore-King), "A Study in Scarlet" (Inspector Lestrade), Terror By Night" (Colonel Moran)

PHILO VANCE

1. (a), (d), (i) & (j) 2. (f) & (h) 3. (e) & (a) 4. (d) 5. (h) 6. (e) 7. (i) & (d) 8. (j) 9. (a), (d), (f), (i), & (j) 10. (h) 11. (g) 12. (f) & (j) 13. (g) 14. (b) 15. (j) 16. (k) 17. (e) 18. (i) 19. (e) 20. (l) & (n) 21. (c) 22. (f) 23. (g) 24. (o) 25. (b)

PERRY MASON

1. (c)   2. (f)   3. (d)   4. (a)   5. (e)   6. (a), (d), (e) & (f)   7. (d) & (f)   8. (e)   9. (c)
10. (d)   11. (b)   12. (a) & (d)   13. (a)   14. (b)   15. (d)   16. (e)   17. (c)

BULLDOG DRUMMOND

Various "Bulldogs"

1. (e)   2. (c)   3. (d)   4. (g)   5. (h)   6. (a)   7. (f)   8. (b)

Leading Ladies

1. (i)   2. (f)   3. (g)   4. (b)   5. (a)   6. (e)   7. (d)   8. (c)   9. (j)   10. (k)   11. (h)

Test Your "Nielsen" Rating

1. (c)   2. (d)   3. (a)   4. (b)

Villains

1. (g)   2. (c)   3. (b)   4. (f)   5. (a)   6. (e)   7. (h)   8. (d)

MR. MOTO

1. (d)   2. (b)   3. (f)   4. (g)   5. (e)   6. (c)   7. (a)   8. (d)   9. Henry Silva

MISS JANE MARPLE

1. (c)   2. (d)   3. (a)   4. (b)

ELLERY QUEEN

1. (a) Bellamy, (b) Gargan, (c) Gargan, (d) Bellamy, (e) Bellamy, (f) Gargan, (g) Bellamy   2. Margaret Lindsay   3. Charley Grapewin   4. James Burke   5. Donald Cook   6. Eddie Quillan

THE SAINT

1. Sanders   2. Hayward   3. Sanders   4. Hayward   5. Sanders   6. Sinclair   7. Sanders
8. Sanders   9. Sinclair

THE FALCON

1. (b)   2. (h)   3. (i)   4. (c)   5. (e)   6. (g)   7. (d)   8. (f) or (i)   9. (a)

HILDEGARDE WITHERS

1. (c), (d), & (f)   2. (a) & (e)   3. (b)   4. all   5. (c)   6. (a)

WEED OUT THE "IMPOSTOR"

1. Lynn Bari   2. Michael Wilding   3. Lee Marvin   4. Tom Helmore   5. Edmund Lowe   6. George Segal   7. Michael Rennie   8. Michael O'Shea   9. Adolphe Menjou   10. Peter Lorre

CREATORS OF DETECTIVE FICTION

1. Gilbert K. Chesterton   2. Earl Derr Biggers   3. Dashiell Hammett   4. Anthony Abbott (Fulton Oursler)
5. Max Marcin   6. Herman Cyril ("Sapper") McNeile   7. Michael Arlen   8. Mickey Spillane   9. Sir Arthur Conan Doyle   10. Mignon G. Eberhart   11. Louis Joseph Vance   12. Raymond Chandler
13. Agatha Christie   14. Erle Stanley Gardner   15. John P. Marquand   16. Mary Roberts Rinehart
17. Agatha Christie   18. Manfred B. Lee & Frederick Dannay ("Ellery Queen" was their pen name.)
19. Leslie Charteris   20. Brett Halliday   21. Dashiell Hammett   22. S. S. Van Dine   23. Stuart Palmer
24. Rex Stout

ALFRED HITCHCOCK

Similar Opening Scenes

1. "Frenzy"   2. "The Girl Was Young" (Title in Great Britain: "Young and Innocent")

Bizarre Happenings

(a) "Topaz"   (b) "Foreign Correspondent"   (c) "Marnie"   (d) "Psycho"   (e) "Suspicion"   (f) "The 39 Steps"   (g) "I Confess"   (h) "Dial M for Murder"   (i) "The Birds"   (j) "Foreign Correspondent"   (k) "Family Plot"   (l) "North By Northwest"

Spine-Chilling Suspense

1. "The Woman Alone" (Title in Great Britain: "Sabotage")   2. "Notorious"   3. "Frenzy"   4. "The Man Who Knew Too Much" (1934 & 1956)   5. "Strangers on a Train"   6. "Shadow of a Doubt"

Cold-Blooded Murders

(a) "Rope"   (b) "Secret Agent"   (c) "Strangers on a Train"

Heart-Pounding Climaxes

1. "Foreign Correspondent"   2. "Saboteur"   3. "North By Northwest"

Casts

(a) Charles Coburn   (b) Wendell Corey   (c) Sir Cedric Hardwicke   (d) Lilli Palmer   (e) Martin Balsam   (f) Louis Calhern   (g) Barry Sullivan

General Questions

1. Norman Lloyd   2. "Murder"   3. Leo G. Carroll   4. "Secret Agent"   5. "Foreign Correspondent"   6. "Blackmail"   7. Richard Todd

ACADEMY AWARD WINNERS & NOMINEES

1. (a) "Bureau of Missing Persons," (b) "Bunny Lake Is Missing," (c) "Nancy Steele Is Missing"   2. W. S. Van Dyke   3. Charles Boyer (starring), Angela Lansbury (supporting)   4. "Foreign Correspondent"   5. Albert Basserman   6. "Rebecca"   7. Laurence Olivier & Joan Fontaine (starring), Judith Anderson (supporting)   8. Bette Davis, David Niven, Maggie Smith, Peter Ustinov, George Kennedy   9. "Sudden Fear"   10. Jack Palance   11. "Rosemary's Baby"   12. "Witness For the Prosecution"   13. "Laura"   14. "Rear Window"   15. "Double Indemnity" (1944) & "Sorry, Wrong Number" (1948)   16. Billy Wilder   17. Michael Chekhov   18. "The Letter"   19. James Stephenson   20. William Wyler   21. "What Ever Happened to Baby Jane?"   22. Victor Buono   23. Janet Leigh   24. "Anatomy of a Murder"   25. "Crossfire"   26. "Hush...Hush, Sweet Charlotte"   27. "Chinatown"   28. "Sleuth"   29. "The Spiral Staircase" (1946) & "The Paradine Case" (1947)   30. Ann Blyth, Eve Arden & Mildred Pierce   31. "Murder on the Orient Express"   32. Robert Montgomery   33. Dame May Whitty   34. (a) "In the Heat of the Night," (b) Rod Steiger, (c) "They Call Me Mister Tibbs!" & "The Organization"

ORIGINALS & REMAKES

1. (a) Ricardo Cortez, Bebe Daniels & Dudley Digges, (b) Warren William, Bette Davis & Alison Skipworth, (c) "Satan Met a Lady"   2. Lionel Atwill (1933), Vincent Price (1953)   3. "The Great Impersonation" 4. "The Mad Room" — Stella Stevens   5. (a) C. Aubrey Smith, Leo Genn, Adolfo Celi, (b) June Duprez, Shirley Eaton, Elke Sommer, (c) Judith Anderson, Dahlia Lavi, Stephane Audran, (d) Barry Fitzgerald, Wilfred Hyde-White, Richard Attenborough, (e) Roland Young, Stanley Holloway, Gert Froebe, (f) Walter Huston, Dennis Price, Herbert Lom, (g) Louis Hayward, Hugh O'Brian, Oliver Reed, (h) Mischa Auer, Fabian, Charles Aznavour, (i) Queenie Leonard, Marianne Hoppe, Maria Rohm, (j) Richard Haydn, Mario Adorf, Alberto de Mendoza   6. Alan Ladd, Brian Donlevy & Richard Denning — "The Glass Key"   7. Peter Lawford — "The Hour of 13"   8. (a) "True Confession" (1937) & "Cross My Heart" (1946), (b) Fred MacMurray (1937) & Sonny Tufts (1946)   9. "Step Down to Terror"   10. "Guilty as Hell" (1932) & "Night Club Scandal" (1937)   11. (a) "I Wake Up Screaming," (b) "Vicki," (c) Jeanne Crain (Grable), Jean Peters (Landis) & Richard Boone (Cregar)   12. (a) Ernest Truex, (b) Edward Arnold, (c) Conrad Veidt   13. (a) Albert Finney, (b) Mona Washbourne, (c) Rosalind Russell 14. (a) Basil Rathbone & Ann Harding, (b) John Hodiak & Sylvia Sidney   15. (a) Lloyd Nolan, (b) George Montgomery, (c) "Time to Kill" (1942); "The Brasher Doubloon" (1947)   16. (a) "Miss Pinkerton," (b) "The Nurse's Secret"   17. (a) "Evelyn Prentice," (b) "Stronger Than Desire," (c) Walter Pidgeon & Virginia Bruce 18. (a) Raymond Hackett, (b) H. B. Warner, (c) Robert Young, (d) Tom Conway   19. "Mr. Moto in Danger Island" 20. (a) Basil Rathbone & Aline MacMahon, (b) Maurice Evans & Ethel Barrymore   21. (a) Robert Donat & Madeleine Carroll, (b) Kenneth More & Taina Elg   22. (a) "The Falcon Takes Over" — George Sanders, (b) "Murder, My Sweet" — Dick Powell, (c) Robert Mitchum, (d) Ward Bond (1942); Mike Mazurki (1944); Jack O'Halloran (1975)   23. (a) Humphrey Bogart (1945); Robert Mitchum (1978), (b) Charles Waldron (1945); James Stewart (1978), (c) Lauren Bacall (older daughter); Martha Vickers (younger daughter), (d) Sarah Miles (older daughter); Candy Clark (younger daughter)   24. The Ritz Brothers   25. (a) Margaret Wycherly, (b) Dame May Whitty

PLOT CAPSULES

1. "Boomerang"   2. "The Dark Corner"   3. "I Wake Up Screaming"   4. "Black Widow"   5. "The Velvet Touch"   6. "Ivy"   7. "Witness to Murder"   8. "Conflict"   9. "Portrait in Black"   10. "Sorry, Wrong Number"   11. "The Night Walker"   12. "Uncle Harry" (also titled "The Strange Affair of Uncle Harry") 13. "The Woman in the Window"   14. "Trent's Last Case"   15. "Chase a Crooked Shadow"   16. "Somebody Killed Her Husband"   17. "Lured"   18. "The Lady in the Car with Glasses and a Gun"   19. "Four Men and a Prayer"   20. "Obsession"   21. "See No Evil"   22. "Night Watch"

TITLE-ROLE QUIZ

1. "Agatha" (Vanessa Redgrave & Dustin Hoffman)   2. "Jane Eyre" (Joan Fontaine & Orson Welles)   3. "The Lodger" (Merle Oberon & George Sanders)   4. "Arabesque" (Sophia Loren & Gregory Peck)   5. "Double Indemnity" (Barbara Stanwyck & Fred MacMurray)   6. "Charade" (Audrey Hepburn & Cary Grant)   7. "Suddenly, Last Summer" (Elizabeth Taylor & Katharine Hepburn)   8. "Hush...Hush, Sweet Charlotte" (Bette Davis & Olivia de Havilland)   9. "Sudden Fear" (Joan Crawford & Jack Palance)   10. "Stage Fright" (Jane Wyman & Marlene Dietrich)   11. "Witness For the Prosecution" (Marlene Dietrich & Tyrone Power)   12. "The Mad Miss Manton" (Barbara Stanwyck & Henry Fonda)   13. "The Female on the Beach" (Joan Crawford & Jeff Chandler)   14. "Above Suspicion" (Joan Crawford & Fred MacMurray)   15. "A Night to Remember" (Loretta Young & Brian Aherne)   16. "Conspirator" (Elizabeth Taylor & Robert Taylor)   17. "Undercurrent" (Katharine Hepburn & Robert Taylor)   18. "The Killers" (Ava Gardner & Burt Lancaster)   19. "Star of Midnight" (Ginger Rogers & William Powell)   20. "Midnight Lace" (Doris Day & Rex Harrison)

UNSCRAMBLE THE "FAST" COUPLES

Robert Montgomery & Rosalind Russell in "Fast and Loose,"   Franchot Tone & Ann Sothern in "Fast and Furious," Melvyn Douglas & Florence Rice in "Fast Company."

AMNESIA VICTIMS

1. Walter Abel & Margot Grahame in "Two in the Dark"   2. Warner Baxter & Margaret Lindsay in "Crime Doctor"   3. Ralph Bellamy & Marian Marsh in "The Man Who Lived Twice" 4. Tom Conway & Ann Rutherford in "Two O'Clock Courage"   5. John Hodiak & Nancy Guild in "Somewhere in the Night"   6. Pat O'Brien & Claire Trevor in "Crack-Up"   7. Gregory Peck & Ingrid Bergman in "Spellbound"   8. William Powell & Hedy Lamarr in "Crossroads"

MATCH THE KILLER WITH THE MOVIE

1. (s)   2. (m)   3. (j)   4. (i)   5. (n)   6. (l)   7. (d)   8. (c)   9. (e)   10. (f)   11. (t)
12. (p)   13. (q)   14. (k)   15. (h)   16. (r)   17. (o)   18. (a)   19. (g)   20. (b)

MATCH THE DETECTIVE WITH THE MOVIE

1. (n) 2. (o) 3. (p) 4. (t) 5. (i) 6. (r) 7. (j) 8. (s) 9. (c) 10. (m) 11. (d)
12. (q) 13. (g) 14. (e) 15. (a) 16. (b) 17. (l) 18. (h) 19. (f) 20. (k)

UNPOPULAR DAMES WHO GOT RUBBED OUT

1. (n) 2. (g) 3. (h) 4. (a) 5. (m) 6. (j) 7. (l) 8. (k) 9. (o) 10. (e) 11. (d)
12. (i) 13. (f) 14. (c) 15. (b)

MURDER, MYSTERY & INTRIGUE INVOLVING TRAINS

1. (f) 2. (i) 3. (s) 4. (r) 5. (n) 6. (h) 7. (e) 8. (a) 9. (m) 10. (d) 11. (c)
12. (v) 13. (k) 14. (g) 15. (u) 16. (w) 17. (j) 18. (b) 19. (p) 20. (l) 21. (o) 22. (t)
23. (q)

MURDER MYSTERIES ABOUT MOVIES & MOVIE STARS

1. (e) 2. (g) 3. (f) 4. (j) 5. (h) 6. (i) 7. (a) 8. (c) 9. (k) 10. (d) 11. (b)

MURDER SET TO MUSIC

1. "Murder at the Vanities"   2. "Nocturne"   3. "Murder on the Blackboard"   4. "Moonlight Murder"
5. "Murder in the Music Hall"   6. "The Phantom Broadcast"   7. "Lady of Burlesque"

"COLORFUL" CRIME CAPERS

1. "The Black Cat" (1941 film)   2. "The Blue Dahlia"   3. "The Blue Gardenia"   4. "The Clouded Yellow"
5. "Green for Danger"   6. "The Green Scarf"   7. "The Red House"   8. "The Secret of the Blue Room"
9. "The White Cockatoo"   10. "The Woman in White"

CREATIVE HOMICIDES

1. "Who Is Killing the Great Chefs of Europe?"   2. "Murders in the Zoo"   3. "Cross Country Cruise"
4. "Doctor X"   5. "The Ex-Mrs. Bradford"

MATCH THE PLAYERS, PARTS & PICTURES

1. (c) "A Woman's Vengeance"   2. (f) "Suddenly, Last Summer"   3. (h) "The Naked Edge"   4. (b) "Affairs of a Gentleman"   5. (g) "Star of Midnight"   6. (a) "The Unsuspected"   7. (d) "The Man Who Cried Wolf"
8. (e) "Murder Man"

CAST OUT THE NON-CAST MEMBER

1. Murray Hamilton   2. Rhys Williams   3. Walter Abel   4. Peter Sellers   5. Ann-Margret   6. Victor Jory   7. Janet Leigh   8. Lee Remick   9. George Sanders   10. Karen Black   11. William Devane 12. Julie Andrews   13. Shelley Duvall   14. June Havoc   15. Bruce Dern   16. Gail Patrick   17. Roy Scheider   18. Gene Hackman   19. Angela Lansbury   20. Gloria DeHaven   21. Peter Cushing 22. Herbert Lom

PICK THE KILLER

1. Basil Rathbone   2. Dana Andrews   3. Ray Collins   4. Robert Elliott   5. Robert Ryan   6. DeWitt Jennings   7. Basil Rathbone   8. Samuel S. Hinds   9. Lee Bowman   10. Lloyd Nolan   11. Rex Harrison   12. Ethel Barrymore   13. Jean Hersholt   14. Arthur Kennedy   15. Ann Harding 16. Pauline Frederick   17. Coleen Gray   18. Richard Conte   19. George Brent   20. Diane Baker 21. Henry Stephenson   22. Tyrone Power   23. Dennis O'Keefe

NOSTALGIA POTPOURRI

1. "The President's Mystery"   2. "The Hidden Eye"   3. "Thunder on the Hill"   4. "The Night Club Lady" (1932) & "The Circus Queen Murder" (1933)   5. "The Witching Hour"   6. "Dangerous Crossing"   7. "70,000 Witnesses"   8. "Rage in Heaven"   9. "The Trial of Vivienne Ware"   10. "The Man in the Net" 11. "Remember Last Night?"   12. "Tomorrow at Seven"   13. "The Longest Night"   14. "Sapphire" 15. "Crime Doctor"   16. "Who Done It?"

MATCH THE CO-STARS WITH THE TITLE

1. (s)   2. (q)   3. (l)   4. (g)   5. (h)   6. (a)   7. (r)   8. (j)   9. (m)   10. (p)   11. (t) 12. (c)   13. (i)   14. (d)   15. (e)   16. (f)   17. (b)   18. (o)   19. (n)   20. (k)

REAL NAMES & "REEL" NAMES

1. "The Cat and the Canary" — Bob Hope & Paulette Goddard   2. Bruce Cabot   3. David Manners   4. Ann Dvorak   5. Gene Raymond   6. Janet Leigh — "Psycho"   7. Barry Fitzgerald — "And Then There Were None"   8. Mae Clarke   9. Tom Conway   10. Helen Twelvetrees   11. George Brent   12. Edward Arnold   13. Penny Singleton   14. Jack Oakie   15. Gail Patrick   16. Lizabeth Scott   17. Richard Dix   18. Melvyn Douglas   19. Susan Hayward   20. Mary Astor

GENERAL KNOWLEDGE TEST

1. Lee Patrick (Effie) & Elisha Cook Jr. (Wilmer)   2. "Frenchman's Creek"   3. Lyle Talbot   4. "Headline Shooter" (Frances Dee), "The Crime of Dr. Hallet" (Josephine Hutchinson)   5. "The List of Adrian Messenger"   6. Robert Montgomery as Philip Marlowe in "Lady in the Lake," George Montgomery as Philip Marlowe in "The Brasher Doubloon"   7. Dashiell Hammett   8. Preston Foster   9. Ricardo Cortez & Donald Woods   10. "The Ninth Guest"   11. "A Feather in Her Hat"   12. "Crime of the Century"   13. "The Son of Monte Cristo" (Joan Bennett), "Strange Woman" (Hedy Lamarr)   14. Dick Powell (Philip Marlowe) & Ricardo Cortez (Perry Mason)   15. "Payment Deferred" (1932) & "The Big Clock" (1948)   16. Ricardo Cortez & Virginia Bruce   17. Warner Oland as Dr. Fu Manchu, Clive Brook as Sherlock Holmes, William Powell as Philo Vance, Eugene Pallette as Sergeant Heath   18. Jacqueline Bisset & Lee Remick in "The Detective," Gena Rowlands & Jill St. John in "Tony Rome," Lainie Kazan & Raquel Welch in "Lady in Cement"

ANSWERS TO PHOTO QUESTIONS

1. "Another Thin Man"   2. "The Black Camel"   3. Ida Lupino   4. Warren William   5. "The Case of the Black Cat"   6. "Bulldog Drummond Escapes"   7. Virginia Field   8. Stringer Davis   9. Margaret Lindsay — "Enemy Agents Meet Ellery Queen"   10. "The Saint in Palm Springs"   11. "The Falcon's Adventure"   12. "Murder on the Blackboard"   13. Warren William — Ida Lupino   14. Margaret Lindsay   15. The Merry Widow Waltz"   16. Frank Albertson   17. Robert Ryan (killer) — Sam Levene (victim)   18. Albert Finney — "Murder on the Orient Express"   19. Norman Jewison   20. Isobel Elsom   21. Rene Clair   22. "Boomerang" — Elia Kazan   23. "Ivy"   24. Myrna Loy   25. Fay Helm   26. "Shaft's Big Score"   27. "The Dark Mirror"   28. "The Suspect"   29. "Lady on a Train"   30. Richard Benjamin   31. "Nocturne"   32. "Green for Danger"   33. "The Ex-Mrs. Bradford"   34. "A Woman's Vengeance"   35. Charles Bickford — "Fallen Angel"   36. Fred Zinnemann   37. Raymond Chandler   38. "Eyes in the Night"   39. "The Thirteenth Letter"   40. Paul Lukas   41. "The Big Clock"